Bitcoin and Cryptocurrency Mining for Beginners

Earn Passive Income and Make Money While You Sleep from Mining Bitcoin, Ethereum and Other Crypto Altcoins

Thomas Kain

OAKRIDGE
PRESS

Contents

Introduction

Do you know that you can make passive income from mining cryptocurrency? In this digital age, it is possible to invest or trade in any asset from any place. Cryptocurrency mining is a good example of an online business you can consider if you are interested in earning extra money. There are thousands of cryptocurrencies available, and they are increasingly getting accepted as an alternative for fiat currencies. Unlike the supply of fiat money, which a central bank controls, a new cryptocurrency is introduced in the blockchain through a sophisticated process known as block mining.

However, cryptocurrency mining can be complicated like any form of online activity. Before you get into this, you should know that it is not a get-rich-quick scheme. The chances of losing or making money are high depending on your approach. If you want to learn different things about cryptocurrency mining, this book is for you.

You will find step-by-step instructions on cryptocurrency mining. First and foremost, it is essential to understand what this business is all about and how to choose the ideal currency to mine. You can mine cryptocurrency without using any fiat currency. The other crucial aspect covered in this book is choosing the right platform or pool to use for mining cryptocurrencies. When selecting a website to do your business, there are several things you should know. This book provides tips and tricks that can help you make informed decisions and hopefully enough knowledge to allow you to make a profit.

This book is easy to understand, and all terms and concepts are explained to benefit all readers. Everything you want to understand about cryptocurrency mining is covered in this book. Many people often face challenges when choosing crypto coins to mine, but this book explains the various mining strategies and their differences. Something that works for someone might not be a good fit for you, and this is why you need to do your own research and make an effort to understand everything surrounding this topic.

You won't find generic information you can get online. You will find well-researched information that will set you on the right path when it comes to mining and crypto.

If you want to get into Bitcoin and cryptocurrency mining today, get this book. Cryptocurrencies might be the future of the internet and the world economy. It's never too late to get into this expansive field.

1

The World of Mining

Are you wondering what Bitcoin mining involves? By now, you must have heard about cryptocurrency trading and the different elements involved. However, Bitcoin is created through computational work, and you can consider this option to earn passive income. This chapter will discuss the key areas that include proof-of-work blockchains, nodes, the public ledger, public keys, hash, private keys, block rewards, and blockchain transaction cost structure.

What Is Bitcoin Mining?
Bitcoin mining is a process by which new cryptocurrencies are introduced into the blockchain. It also plays a critical role in

helping networks confirm new transactions and maintaining the blockchain ledger. Sophisticated hardware is used for mining, and it can solve extremely complex computational problems. In other words, mining bitcoins works just as mining for silver or gold, which requires physical effort. Crypto miners will receive virtual tokens that will exist only in the ledger of the Bitcoin blockchain.

Cryptocurrency mining is costly and often sporadically rewarding. However, crypto mining still commands a magnetic appeal to investors since miners will get rewards for their work. Miners are paid for their work as auditors, and they also verify the legitimacy of blockchain transactions by including them in the distributed ledger. Bitcoin verification also helps in preventing issues like double-spending by bad actors. Digital platforms can be easily manipulated, and this is why the digital ledger must be regularly updated by debiting one account and crediting the other whenever a transaction is performed.

There is a possibility of double-spending with digital currency where the Bitcoin owner can spend the same coin twice. This is not possible with fiat currency, but the cryptocurrency holder can make a copy of the digital token they have. Crypto mining prevents this scenario by monitoring and legitimizing all transactions to ensure their validity. The reward miners get an incentive that motivates many individuals to try Bitcoin mining.

Mining Hardware

You should invest in appropriate hardware if you want to mine competitively. For instance, you will need a powerful computer such as a graphics processing unit (GPU) or an application-specific integrated circuit (ASIC). These components can cost you a few hundreds to thousands of dollars. However, you need to check whether mining is the right fit for you before investing your time and equipment.

While individuals can mine Bitcoin, many miners choose to work in pools. It becomes easier to find solutions to complex puzzles when separate computing powers work collectively. Mining bitcoins using a personal computer can be a futile exercise. Therefore, you need to check if you can meet all the requirements before mining cryptocurrency.

Proof-of-Work Blockchains

The main feature of Bitcoin is its decentralization which implies that it operates without the intervention of a central authority like a bank or government. All the records and transactions are stored on a network of users called a blockchain. However, without a central authority to control cryptocurrency, the issue of manipulation is a cause for concern. To avoid this, proof of work is the answer.

Proof-of-work is a mechanism designed to ensure that all the participants within a network, miners, use alphanumeric codes or hashes to verify all Bitcoin transactions before adding them to the block in the blockchain. Like mining precious minerals, crypto mining follows the same method, but it will lead to the release of new coins into circulation. Miners need to use machines to solve complex mathematical puzzles to get rewards with new coins. Cryptographic hashes are used to secure digital data transferred on a public network.

Each block will use a hash function that links with the previous block to form an unbroken chain of blocks. The participants on the network can easily verify the validity of blocks to check whether the miners properly solved the hash to get their reward. Essentially, proof of work relates to how miners prove they have put in the necessary work to develop the block of transactions that can be added to the blockchain. Cryptocurrency mining is tamper-proof since no individual miner can alter the data stored in the network. More importantly, all the participants can verify the transactions to identify suspicious activities within the network.

Cryptocurrency mining is a competition where miners try to outdo each other to be the first to solve complex cryptographic puzzles to add the next block to the blockchain to receive compensation. The winning miner can only get compensation after the other systems in the network verify that the solution is valid through proof of work. This method of verifying new coins has proved to work well for more than a decade now. However, proof of work consumes a significant amount of energy. It can lead to energy consumption being equivalent to that of a small nation, and a lot of electronic waste is also recorded in the form of mining units that will be discarded eventually.

Nodes

A node is known as a point of connection within a specific data communication network. Each accessible device on the network is a node, and their descriptions depend on the type of network. For example, any home appliance that can receive or transmit information over a network is regarded as a node. The purpose of nodes is to communicate, receive, and store information or pass it to other nodes. A scanner will create images and send them to the computer for further processing. A router also organizes data from the internet and distributes it to different devices connected to the network.

The concept of nodes applies to different situations. In the world of digital currency, a node is viewed as a computer that connects to any cryptocurrency network. Your computer should be linked to other devices in the network to perform transactions. The node can support the network, and this is done through validation and relaying transactions. The node will also get a copy of the entire blockchain.

There are different categories of nodes which include full nodes and lightweight nodes. As the name suggests, full nodes enforce all the rules of Bitcoin, whereas lightweight nodes are primarily meant for ease of use. However, lightweight nodes are the most popular form available on the network, even though full nodes constitute the backbone. A simple box can collect inputs, and it can do something to the data to produce an output. This box is known as a node, and a collection of several nodes is called a network.

The nodes use specific rules to bind to each other. For instance, member nodes within a specific blockchain network use a consensus protocol instead of relying on third parties to mediate the transactions. The nodes will agree on cryptographic hashes, ledger content, and digital signatures to ensure the authenticity and integrity of all transactions.

On some networks, a node can only have one input while others consist of three or more inputs. In cryptocurrencies, the nodes commonly involved are transaction data (a record), hash pointer, and timestamp. All the blocks are linked in chronological order, also known as a blockchain. Each blockchain comes with smart contracts, and they operate automatically. They have lines of computer code, and the contracts do not need any intermediary like a lawyer or notary to function. When you execute a cryptocurrency transaction, the nodes in the network will take care of everything, and you do not need to do anything since everything is recorded automatically.

There should be a replication of data in the cryptocurrency network since it is stored across all the nodes within the network. Transaction data cannot be stored in one node, and this is why it is called a distributed ledger. Data replication is vital since it makes it difficult for the blocks to be manipulated. It also makes it impossible to perform a successful cyber-attack.

Nodes in a blockchain provide a strong defense mechanism to protect data since a hacker would need to attack all the blocks simultaneously. This is impossible since a blockchain can have tens of thousands of nodes. There is no way a hacker can attack all these components simultaneously. In other words, the system eliminates the fear of hacking or other cyberattacks, which are common when individuals perform an online transaction. Dealing damage to mass-scale data is almost impossible since no single attack can impact the entire network.

The Public Ledger

A public ledger can be viewed and verified publicly, and it derives its name from the old system of keeping records and other vital information like news, prices, and analyses. Similarly, cryptocurrency-based blockchain systems rely on the same record-keeping and public verification mechanisms. In other words, a cryptocurrency public ledger is meant to keep records. It maintains the participants' cryptocurrency balances, their identities, and records of every transaction performed between network members.

Since a cryptocurrency is an encrypted and decentralized digital currency that can facilitate the exchange of value by transferring tokens between the participants within the network, it is vital to enhance security in all transactions. Security threats like hacking are real, and they can impact blockchain users if the proper security measures are not taken. This is where a public ledger becomes useful. It keeps the details of transactions and ensures they are inaccessible to unauthorized people. A public ledger can verify all the details required before a transaction is processed.

A transaction is verified by the two parties involved in a normal banking system. If you send money to someone, your bank will verify the balances and everything to check if it is possible to process the transaction. The recipient's bank will also do the same, and the bank records are only accessible to authorized people. No one else can access the details of transactions between two parties. Public ledgers work similarly. The details of a cryptocurrency transaction can only be verified by the two parties involved. However, the difference is that there is no central authority, and they may not know the parties' identity. Transactions can only be processed after verification of the sender's liquidity and verification of their details; otherwise, they will be discarded if they do not meet the requirements.

A public ledger is regarded as a data management or a storage system in terms of physical banking. On the other hand, a blockchain is a kind of public ledger consisting of a series of blocks where transaction details are recorded for verification and authentication by authorized network participants. The storage of confirmed transactions in public ledgers starts with creating the cryptocurrency. All new currencies are added to the blockchain by the miners.

Select network participants, also called full nodes, are responsible for copying the whole ledger using their devices that are connected to the cryptocurrency network. The public ledger is distributed as the participants contribute to the blockchain network activities to keep it functional and agile. However, thousands of participants keep a copy of the ledger, and they know the state of the network regarding the holders of the crypto tokens. They also know the exact number of tokens held by different participants in the network. All the transactions are recorded in the ledger to prevent issues like double-spending.

A public ledger consists of intrinsic features such as encryption, consensus algorithms, and reward mechanisms to protect the participants' identities. Only genuine transactions can be performed on the network to maximize security. If you want to send Bitcoin to someone, you only need to broadcast the encrypted transaction number or wallet address for the two parties involved. You can conceal the amount depending on the configuration of the network. An internal digital signature will ensure that only the person with appropriate crypto coins can conduct the transactions from their accounts or wallets.

All the full nodes on the network will see the broadcast transaction and verify it. They can also update the public ledger records on different nodes part of the cryptocurrency network. There are concerns about the use of public ledgers, although they have several advantages. For example, the working mechanism of the blockchain is to record every single transaction that occurs on the network.

However, balancing the detailed history while scaling the ability to process the increasing number of transactions can be problematic. There are concerns that keeping a public ledger with every transaction record can allow security agencies, governments, and hackers to track network participants. This will expose the anonymity of the blockchain participants. Other security agencies are already accused of trying to track down Bitcoin owners. Public ledger-based cryptocurrency is not immune to hacking attempts like any other online transaction.

Hash

A hash is a mathematical function that can convert an input of variable length into an encrypted output consisting of a fixed length. You cannot use hashes to reverse engineer an input from a hashed output. In other words, the hash functions are one way, and you cannot undo the action you have already performed. If you apply the hash function on the same data, the hash will be similar. Hashing is also crucial to blockchain management, and it provides the demands required to solve some computations involved.

A hash has a fixed length to make it impossible for someone who may try to guess the length to crack the blockchain. It is the foundation of the blockchain network and is often developed based on the data available in the block header. A cryptographic hash function consists of message-passing capabilities of hash functions and security properties. Hash functions mainly involve data structures in various computing systems for tasks like authenticating information and checking the integrity of the messages. They are not easily decipherable, although they can be polynomial-time which makes them considered cryptographically weak.

Cryptographic hash functions enhance security features, making it difficult to detect the details of senders and recipients. They also exhibit three properties that include the following:

- They can be hidden, which makes it challenging to guess the input value of the hash function from the output
- No two hashes can be used to map the same output hash
- It should not be easy to select an input that will provide a predefined output. The input should be obtained from wide distribution.

Hashes are extensively used for online security because of their features. They are mainly used to protect passwords, check the integrity of download files, and detect data breaches.

Hashing plays a critical role in cryptocurrencies. A blockchain is the backbone of any cryptocurrency, which is a global ledger created by connecting different blocks of transaction data. A blockchain only has validated transactions, preventing fraudulent activities like double spending of the same currency. The resulting encrypted value is called a hash, and it involves figures and letters that are different from the original data. When mining cryptocurrency, you should work with this hash.

Hashing requires the miner to process data using a mathematical function that will result in an output with a fixed length to increase security. Any person who may try to decrypt the hash will not be able to tell the length of the input by looking at the output. The data available in the header can help you solve complex mathematical problems. In each block header, you will find a version number, the hash used in the previous block, timestamp, the nonce, the hash of the Merkel, and the target hash.

The miner will specifically focus on the nonce comprising a string of numbers. The nonce will be appended to the hashed contents found in the previous block that is then hashed. If the new hash is equal to or less than the target hash, it will be accepted as a solution. The miner receives the reward, and the new block will be added to the blockchain.

Public Keys

Both public and private keys are an integral part of all cryptocurrencies. These keys allow you to send or receive cryptocurrency without the intervention of a third party like a central bank to verify the transaction. The keys constitute a public-key cryptography (PKC) framework, and you can use them to send cryptocurrency anywhere, anytime, and to any person.

A public key is designed to allow you to receive cryptocurrency transactions, and the cryptographic code is paired with a private key. Anyone can send a transaction to a public key, but the recipient will require a private key to prove they are the owner of the cryptocurrency sent. A public key that receives transactions is an address consisting of a shortened form of the public key. You can share your public key without any worries since you will need a private key to unlock the funds. In other words, a public key is more like an email address. However, the email can only be accessible to a person with a password.

Private Keys

A private key, just like a password, gives you access to spend the funds sent to your public address. You can use it to prove ownership of the funds, but, like any other personal identification number (PIN) or password, you must not share it with anyone. A private key comes in different forms, including the following:

- A QR code
- A binary code with 256 characters
- 64 digit hexadecimal code
- Mnemonic phrase

It can be observed that a private key is an astronomically large figure regardless of its form. There is a good reason behind the length of the private key. A public key can be generated using a private key, but you cannot do the opposite.

Where Do You Get Your Private Keys?

You can get your private keys in a cryptocurrency wallet, and this is typically desktop or mobile software or another specialized hardware device. Remember, your private key is not on the cryptocurrency blockchain network. If you choose to keep cryptocurrency on an exchange, you will be entrusting it to keep your private keys the same way you can trust your bank to keep your valuable possessions. Once you transfer your cryptocurrency from an exchange, you will be in control of the keys. Given the nature of cryptocurrency wallets, you will not handle the private keys since the wallets automatically manage them for you. You will get a seed phrase that can encode your private key.

To complete any transaction on the blockchain, you need to sign it digitally. When someone sends you a transaction, they follow the steps below.

- A public key is used to encrypt the transaction, which can only be decrypted by the private key accompanying it
- The transaction will be signed using a private key to prove that it has not been altered
- The accompanying public key can be used to verify the authenticity of the transaction

When you receive the transaction, you should digitally sign it to prove you are the owner of the funds. Nodes can check and authenticate all the transactions automatically. If the transaction is not authenticated, the network will reject it. A mined and authentic transaction is irreversible on the blockchain.

Public and private keys are fundamental to understanding the functions of cryptocurrency transactions. It is stored on the blockchain, which will help anyone verify you as the currency owner. Depending on various factors, you can hold your private keys or entrust them with a custodian. If you choose to keep your keys, you can get modern hard drive wallets and never share them with anyone. For a custodial solution, you should make sure you choose a reputable and trusted company that prioritizes security and regulation.

Blockchain Transaction Cost Structure

Blockchain provides a unique opportunity for financial institutions to improve their operations. It can also change our lives immensely by providing new opportunities to transform how we collaborate and interact in different activities with better security. A disruptive technology like the emergency of cryptocurrencies has improved the way transactions are conducted between parties. For instance, a blockchain is a distributed ledger that provides a reliable, immutable, and shared view of transactions and property records between the parties involved in an untrusted environment.

Blockchain has unique features that allow institutions to operate quickly and more cheaply. It also reduces the chances of errors, leading to fewer risks, limited vulnerability to cyber-attacks, and lower capital requirements. Financial institutions are most likely to be affected by this kind of technology, which may impact the global economic system long-term. Blockchain can reshape the market structure, product features, and customer experience. It can also drive major change, and the potential in the financial services sector is huge. Blockchain technology can go a long way in achieving substantial cost savings across capital markets, payments, trade services, and investment management.

Studies indicate that distributed ledger technology can reduce financial services costs by US$15 billion to $20 billion per year by 2022. Many companies will get the opportunity to reduce the demand for manual aggregating, sharing, or amending data. Regulating and reporting or auditing documents can also become easier since it will require less manual processing. This will help employees to focus on core activities that will add value to their operations. Post-trade settlement and reconciliation are good examples of expensive and time-consuming activities that can be addressed by adopting blockchain technology by large financial institutions.

With blockchain technology, financial institutions can share common digital data keep track of clearing and settlement of securities transactions outside their databases. For instance, the technology can provide smart contracts for insurance companies. This involves a digitally signed computable agreement between two or more parties capable of initiating specific actions. Blockchain helps make P2P insurance trustworthy and transparent for the consumers since it does not involve any central authority which controls the operations. The smart contracts can initiate payouts for all the insured flight tickets when delays or cancellations are reported.

Blockchain technology can also facilitate the claims management process by ensuring the payment of valid claims only. The main benefit of this system is the reduction or prevention of fraud since the network will reject multiple claims for one event. If the claim has already been paid, the network has the information. Storing all the details on the ledger also helps insurers identify suspicious activities and improve their security. Home appliances or other electronic devices can have insurance policies administered by smart contracts within a blockchain network in the digital age. It will automatically detect damage and trigger the repair process as well as claims and payment processes. Smart contract car insurance is embedded in the vehicle, and it will gather a variety of information such as driving style, speed, time of drive, road risk, weather, and traffic conditions. The system will determine the insurance premiums based on reliable data to eliminate losses that false claims can cause.

Financial institutions can also capitalize on blockchain technology to avoid lagging behind other innovative companies. It provides a unique opportunity to transform the way institutions and their customers interact and collaborate in different activities. However, since this is still new technology, there are still outstanding points related to regulation, security, and scalability that should be addressed. There is a need for a few more years before the technology is adopted as mainstream.

Block Rewards

Many people choose to mine Bitcoin to earn a profit which comes as a reward for solving complex equations. This is possible if you use the right tools and the necessary resources. The second reason for mining Bitcoin is to help different people learn about how cryptocurrencies work.

Bitcoin block rewards are new coins offered to cryptocurrency miners when they solve the equations and create a new block of valid and verified transactions. Networks of computers are utilized for this function, and the competing miners will verify every newly created block. The number of coins you get after solving a specific problem will halve after creating 210,000 blocks or approximately every four years. It is anticipated that the block rewards will hit zero around 2140.

Essentially, the purpose of block rewards is to provide an incentive to the miners to facilitate and validate all the transactions. The blockchain acts like a decentralized ledger that cannot be altered once created. The miners should verify all the transactions and maintain the ledger up to date. Therefore, block rewards are the payment offered to the crypto miners for doing this kind of work.

Bitcoin was designed in such a way that new coins are constantly created, and the challenges of the math problems are adjusted every two weeks. The main competitor of Bitcoin is Ethereum, and it also depends on block rewards to create new coins by offering incentives to the miners. Ethereum miners get a digital token known as "ether," and it is offered every time a miner successfully solves a mathematical problem. They are also awarded transaction fees. There is no limit in terms of the number of Ethereum tokens that can be created, unlike Bitcoin. The number of blocks in Ethereum is bigger than in Bitcoin since they can be created in seconds instead of 10 minutes.

Unlike fiat currency, the supply of Bitcoin is limited to reduce or control inflation. It was designed in such a way that there would only be 21 million coins. For this reason, the size of block rewards for Bitcoin is halved after the development of 210,000 blocks which usually takes an average of about four years. By May 2020, there were already 18.7 million bitcoins in supply, or about 90% of the intended supply. By May 2140, block reward is expected to reach zero, and mining will no longer be profitable.

This should not deter you from mining Bitcoins since you need to do it properly if you want to enjoy better rewards. Make sure you have the appropriate hardware and consider a strong internet bandwidth with unlimited usage. Access to low-cost power such as solar energy can help you gain considerable profits if you reduce operational costs. Going solo can be problematic when you decide to venture into Bitcoin mining. Some minders join forces to improve their chances and earn rewards. The members will share the profits and pay a membership fee. Teamwork is believed to be effective, and this can help you earn some rewards if you don't want to invest money in cryptocurrency.

Bitcoin mining plays a crucial role in validating and confirming all new transactions in the blockchain. This prevents issues like double-spending by unscrupulous actors. Mining also introduces new coins into the system. The process of mining is based on a complex puzzle that requires the development of proof of work (PoW) which is power-intensive. Before you start mining, make sure you have the appropriate resources.

Key Takeaways

- Mining is a process of introducing new coins into the system, and it involves computational work.
- You can earn cryptocurrency through mining and without investing money in it.
- The miners receive rewards for completing verified transactions or blocks, which are then added to the blockchain. The rewards are offered to the miners who first discover the solutions to complex hashing puzzles.
- You need a graphics processing unit (GPU) or application-specific integrated circuit (ASIC) to start mining.
- Bitcoins should be mined because they are digital records that can be exposed to the risk of counterfeiting, copying, or double-spending. Therefore, mining helps resolve these challenges by making the process resource-intensive and extremely expensive.
- A public ledger has intrinsic features such as consensus algorithms, encryption, and reward mechanisms to protect the participants. Only verifiable transactions can be performed on a network to maximize security.
- Mining plays a role in validating and confirming new transactions on the blockchain. This is vital since no central authority like a bank or government controls the blockchain.
- Only a holder of valid public and private keys can access the funds sent through a network. The keys are used to verify and prove ownership of the account. All transactions are kept in a public ledger, and they are not accessible to people without keys to access the network.

- Proof-of-work is another effective mechanism designed to ensure all the miners have appropriate code hashes to verify all new coins and transactions before they are added to the blockchain.
- If used properly, blockchain technology can significantly lower the cost of transacting in different sectors. It eliminates the need for an intermediary to facilitate a transaction between two entities.
- The rewards for block mining vary depending on the cryptocurrency. With Bitcoin, the miners should follow a specific set of rules, and the compensation is halved every time a new block is added to the network. It is expected that mining will no longer be profitable by 2140.

The next chapter will focus on the most popular coins mined.

2

Coins We're Mining

If you're reading this book, then you're likely thinking of getting into cryptocurrency mining. Chances are you're also wondering which coins are best to mine. Before making this decision, there is plenty to consider, including what you want to achieve with mining. For most people, the answer is pretty simple. They want to make an immediate profit. Others, however, want to take up mining as a hobby and are looking to make it a long-term source of income.

Many people also take up an interest in mining cryptocurrency because they want to be part of securing the network. This is especially true for many Bitcoin enthusiasts.

Although they wouldn't be getting any direct profit from it, their contribution helps keep the network running and decentralized.

Mining Difficulty

If you're hoping to get into crypto mining for profit, either short-term or long-term, there's a concept we need to cover first: mining difficulty. The difficulty of guessing the block's hash on a cryptocurrency network is referred to as mining difficulty. This process is necessary to make sure that not too many coins get released too quickly. Even when numerous miners can be found on the mining network, keeping a constant rate means that the mining difficulty increases. However, if there are just a few miners, the problems will be relatively easy to solve. A coin's mining difficulty also affects its mining profitability. If you're using hardware limited to GPU units, you should go for a coin with a lower mining difficulty.

Profitability

If you're opting for no more than short-term profitability, you must stay on top of any changes in the mining conditions for various projects. The mining difficulty is always changing, so what generates profit today may not necessarily work tomorrow. This is why you need to learn about the various mining options, which we will be exploring in this chapter to determine what you can mine. Instead of having someone tell you which coin to mine, you should do your own research when it comes to which coins to mine. This way, you can comfortably switch from one coin to the other so you can mine the ones with the highest profitability at that period.

Numerous mining profitability calculators will help you check each cryptocurrency's profitability. Most of them offer huge selections of altcoins you can choose from. The calculator will ask you for your mining rigs' total hashing power. Note that every CPU or GPU has a different rate. You will also have to provide the total amount of power your rigs consume. You can probably find this information on the mining hardware's specification page. You will have to contact your electricity provider to find out the exact price of electricity. You will have to look it up in kilowatt-hour. Some calculators may ask you for your mining pool fee too. The calculator will automatically generate the expected amounts of profit you can make per day, week, month, and year.

If you're looking into cryptocurrency mining as a long-term endeavor, you will have to look at the coin's long-term potential when deciding on a coin to mine. You may find that a coin isn't that attractive in terms of mining profitability. However, your efforts can be a great way to collect as many coins as possible before the currency's price increases with more adoption in the future. Ethereum is a great example of projects with promising long-term potential, even though they may not have high mining profitability today.

There is one important thing to keep in mind. If you determine the coin you want to mine based on its long-term potential, first determine if you can get better use out of your mining rig by mining a different coin first to trade for your long-term project. However, this requires more work and effort since you will need to trade the coins you have and stay on top of the most profitable coins to mine. You will also have to pay for trading and transaction fees.

This chapter will explain the proof-of-stake consensus protocol and explain why we will not be mining the cryptocurrencies that use this protocol to validate crypto transactions. We will also cover the most commonly mined coins. This chapter will mainly focus on coins like Bitcoin,

Ethereum (before switching to proof-of-stake), Dogecoin, Litecoin, Zcash, and Monero. You will find out why these coins are the best ones to work with. Finally, we will explore and understand the various use cases of Ethereum, such as NFTs, DeFi, and DAOs.

Proof-of-Stake Consensus Protocol

Proof-of-stake consensus protocol is a mechanism cryptocurrencies use to process transactions and generate new blocks in the blockchain. A consensus mechanism or protocol is a means of validating entries into a dispersed database. This process is necessary to ensure and maintain the security of the database. As you already know, in the world of cryptocurrency, this database is called a blockchain. So, in that case, the consensus protocol is used to keep the blockchain secure.

How It Works

Proof-of-stake consensus protocol diminishes the amount of computational or technical work the verification of transactions or blocks needs to keep a blockchain and the cryptocurrency secure. This consensus mechanism changes the process of the verification of the blocks using the coin owners' machines. The coins of the miner are used as collateral for the opportunity to validate blocks.

This protocol enables cryptocurrency owners to stake their coins and generate their own validator notes. This is called staking, and it refers to the process of pledging coins so they can be used to verify transactions. The crypto owners of the stake coins are then called validators. When staked, the coins get locked up. However, the validator can easily take them out of stake if they wish to trade them.

28

When a block of transactions is ready to be processed, the protocol randomly selects a validator node to mine, review, or validate the block. While the proof-of-stake mechanism relies on randomization, the proof-of-work protocol is competition-based. The transactions in the block are then checked for accuracy by the validator. If they are accurate, the validator adds the block to the blockchain, and then they receive a reward in cryptocurrency for their contribution. Each block is validated by more than one person and is only finalized when a certain number of validators decide that it's accurate. If a validator passes an inaccurate transaction to the blockchain, they get penalized and lose some of the coins held at stake.

Let's take Cardano, which uses proof-of-stake as an example. Any owner of Cardano can easily stake their coins and create their own validator node. When Cardano has to verify blocks of transactions, Ouroboros, the protocol that it uses, randomly selects a validator. The validator then checks the block. If the information is accurate, they add it to the blockchain and are rewarded with more Cardano.

Not all proof-of-stake mechanisms use the same process to validate blocks. For instance, while Ethereum still uses a proof-of-work consensus protocol, it will soon switch to a proof-of-stake mechanism. When that happens, they plan on using shards for the submissions of transactions. This means that validators will verify the transactions and pass them off to a shard block. To become finalized, at least 128 validators will be required to attest to every shard block, which will be known as a committee. Once they are validated, and therefore the block is created, ⅔ of the validators have to agree on the validation of the transaction. Only then the block gets closed. So, unlike in the proof-of-work consensus protocol, the proof-of-stake mechanism is more collaborative than a competitive validation process. The validation process is shared across a cryptocurrency network.

Aims of Proof-of-Stake

You are probably wondering why the proof-of-work consensus protocol is designed that way. The main aim behind it is to be more environmentally sustainable and decrease scalability. There are concerns surrounding the harmful impact the proof-of-work mechanism leaves on the environment, especially since it's competition-based, which urges people to search for ways to place themselves at an advantage. For example, while those who mine Bitcoin earn more of it by verifying blocks and transactions, they still use fiat currency to pay for rent, electricity, and other operating costs. This means that they're using up energy in exchange for earning more cryptocurrency. It must be noted that the amount of energy that mining proof-of-work cryptocurrency takes up leaves a huge impact on the factors surrounding profitability and pricing in the market. Additionally, the environmental factors must be accounted for, considering that the entire proof-of-work process consumes as much energy as the average small country.

The proof-of-stake protocol is designed to fix these issues because it actively replaces computational power with staking. So, the network's randomized selection determines a person's mining ability instead of relying on hardware, which consumes plentiful amounts of energy. Peercoin was the first cryptocurrency to implement a proof-of-stake consensus protocol shortly after Blackcoin, Nxt, and ShadowCoin.

PoS Security

When PoS (proof-of-stake) is in place, there is always a concern surrounding the 51% attack. This type of attack is a threat when someone controls or owns 51% of the cryptocurrency because they can alter the blockchain. This can either be an individual or a group of people who own that percentage of the staked cryptocurrency. Many people suggest that this attack is very unlikely to occur because it would cost a lot for someone to possess 51% of the staked cryptocurrency. Additionally, those who try to conduct a 51% attack to alter a block would wind up losing all of their staked coins. This makes miners more likely to act righteously and ethically. Many other security features of this protocol are not made available to the public.

PoS Mining Power

The number of coins a validator is staking determines the mining power in PoS. Generally speaking, those who have more coins at stake are more likely to be selected to add new blocks. As we mentioned above, each PoS mechanism works differently, and this also applies to the process in which it selects validators. There's typically a randomization aspect involved in the procedure. However, the process may also depend on other elements, including the time period in which validators have staked their coins.

Even though anyone who stakes cryptocurrency can be selected as a validator, the chances are exceptionally low if you're staking a relatively small amount. For instance, your chances to be selected as a validator would be 0.001% of your staked amount of coins. This is why many miners prefer to join staking pools. The owner of the staking pool is the one who creates the validator node, so a group of miners pools their coins together. This grants them a greater chance of winning more blocks. The rewards are then divided among the participants of the pool. Many pool owners may require a small entry fee.

PoS vs. PoW

As you are already aware, proof-of-stake and proof-of-work (PoW) are the two most popular consensus protocol types used by cryptocurrencies. Early cryptocurrencies like Bitcoin referred to PoW as the go-to mechanism of choice. However, upon the introduction of PoS through Peercoin in 2012, this protocol became a popular choice among various altcoins. As we mentioned above, the greatest difference between PoS and PoW is their energy consumption. Miners with cryptocurrencies that use proof-of-work are required to solve highly complex mathematical problems, which creates a competitive approach. The first miner able to solve the problems gets to validate the transactions or add them to the blockchain and receives coins as a reward in return. This process involves numerous mining devices across the globe computing the same problems and consuming huge amounts of energy. While proof-of-stake is more advantageous, it still has its downsides in terms of the environmental impact. Here are the pros and cons of the PoS consensus protocol:

Pros of PoS
- It is more energy-efficient than PoW.
- It offers a fast and relatively inexpensive means of transaction processing.
- You don't need specialized equipment to validate PoS transactions.

Cons of PoS

- The PoS consensus protocol is not as proven when it comes to issues of security as PoW.
- Validators with a large number of coins can easily influence and alter the verification of transactions.
- Some cryptocurrencies that use a PoS consensus protocol require you to lock up your staked coins for a minimum amount of time before you can participate in any mining or validating activities.

Examples of PoS Altcoins

- **Cardano**: it is a blockchain platform primarily driven by research. This altcoin prioritized sustainability and values security.
- **Tezos:** it is a programmable blockchain. This altcoin incorporates an on-chain mechanism for upgrades, which is a feature that eases adaptability.
- **Algorand:** it is an altcoin that utilizes a two-tier blockchain structure. This design provides incredibly high processing speeds of 1000 transactions per second.

Why PoW Is Better than PoS

In this book, we will be focusing on mining cryptocurrencies that use proof-of-work consensus protocols rather than ones that use proof-of-stake, and here's why:

A PoW consensus protocol is a subjective system comprising smart contracts, accounts, and balances. It is built upon an objective physical or tangible base that consumes energy to generate data blocks. These blocks of information are then added to the blockchain, which is incredibly secure. This anchoring of structure allows the subjective system to obtain orders of great prominence in a more objective and, therefore, more secure manner than if it were not anchored to a PoW physical foundation. To tackle scalability issues, PoS gives up the physical base of the PoS protocol. This makes PoS highly subjective.

PoS consensus protocols are not systems that consume large amounts of energy to build data blocks and secure them. Instead, they build transaction data in batches and link them in a way that makes them seem like blockchains. It merely copies the actual design of the blockchain, which plays no role in increasing or reducing objectivity and therefore doesn't ensure security in the distributed ledgers.

The subjective layer of the blockchains (PoW) and distributed ledgers (PoS) is where the beneficial features and functional aspects lie. It's comparable to how fiat monetary systems are managed by their environments. But instead of being controlled by the central bank or governments, the subjective layer that comprises smart contents, balances, applications, and rules, can be altered if the participants agree on the changes. What PoW does is that it anchors this subjective and volatile layer on a physical foundation. Since PoS lacks this anchor, they are no different than any traditionally managed system. This is a problem because all the choices and designs, like pools, slots, elected block producers, and voting, would still be skewed toward subjective human incentives and not objective security.

Fault Tolerance

The number of nodes present in a distributed network that can disturb the system if they act unethically and send corrupt information to other participants is referred to by fault tolerance. Before the creation of Bitcoin, the fault tolerance of distributed systems was 33%. PoW, on the other hand, achieved a fault tolerance of 50%. This was achieved not by solving the core fault tolerance issue but by getting around it. PoW gets miners to send an external physical signal to the nodes in the network, which increases security. PoS remains at a fault tolerance of 33%.

Fork Choice

The decision rule participants must use when they are presented with more than one chain upon joining it for the first time when it splits, or if they leave and rejoin is referred to by fork choice. Since PoW is an external physical system, it allows for an objective fork choice, presenting the longest PoW chain. It's objective because the longest chain can be established only through the whole network's computing power. Since PoS systems don't need this much objective quantity to determine the correct chain, they rely on the participants' subjective decision-making process. To decide which chain to follow, they consult off-chain developers, block explorers, miners, etc., in any of the cases we mentioned above.

Costliness and Proxy for Value

Fiat currency is very expensive to produce to ensure that it isn't forged. This is the same with PoW. The costliness of the tokens is provided through the high costs miners need to incur through electricity and data centers to build blocks. This costliness acts as a proxy for the value of the tokens in the greater economy. In PoS, there is no objective costliness because the validators and nodes write the accounts and balances. This means that it lacks an objective measure of value.

Accumulated Work

In PoW blockchains, miners have to work on a block-by-block basis. This makes it impossible for unethical nodes to disrupt the existing blocks. It also ensures the accumulation of work throughout the building process of the chains. This means that even the blocks that are further back in the chain are very hard to alter or forge by attackers. For instance, to reverse the entire chain, you need 100% of the Bitcoin network's current hashing power and around 340 days. However, with PoS distributed ledgers, this process can be done in just a few minutes.

The Location of the Block Creator

The block creators are separated from the ledger in PoW because the network of nodes that hold it comprises the smart contracts, balances, and accounts mined through an external process. This independence grants the miners more security. Full node operators in charge of maintaining the ledger can delink from block creators if they become corrupted or disrupt the network.

In retrospect, since the participants need to deposit stakes in the ledgers in PoS, this makes them on the internal database. This means that all the other nodes that maintain the network's ledger are not independent of block creators. The node operators are stuck with the validator. This makes PoS not censorship-resistant.

Social Scalability

Since PoW is an objective system, it doesn't exclude any participants who hold a bias toward a certain group of people. The system is socially scalable across the globe. PoS systems, on the other hand, will possibly end up leaving the system in control of a few validators which can be easily identified. They will likely exclude groups of people upon external pressure or based on personal biases, convictions, or preferences.

The Top Most Commonly Mined Coins

Vertcoin

Vertcoin is an ASIC-resistant cryptocurrency. This means that its mining algorithm and protocol are built to make it impossible to use ASIC machines to mine the coin. You can make a daily profit of $4.90 at a $0.10 kWh electricity rate at a mining hash rate of 2.50 mh/s and power consumption of 450 watts. The algorithm of the coin, Verthash, is built to create one block every 2 minutes and 24 seconds. The reward for one block is 12.5 Vertcoins.

Bitcoin

If you're using an ASIC, Bitcoin would be the most profitable mining option. However, it isn't really profitable, even if you use a mining pool with a GPU. However, you can still mine using pools, like Nicehash, that allow you to get rewarded in Bitcoin for contributing the hash rate to mine other altcoins. According to Nicehash, you can earn a daily profit of 0.000125 BTC to 0.00022200 BTC if you use NVIDIA RTX 3090, NVIDIA RTX 3080, NVIDIA RTX A5000, NVIDIA Tesla A100, and NVIDIA CMP 90HX to mine Bitcoin. This a daily profit of around $6 to $11 at $0.1 electricity cost. If you'd like to do solo mining, you can build a rig. You can also connect a single GPU or the rig to a pool.

Monero

Monero is among the easiest altcoins to mine using a GPU. Many people also try to mine it on VCPU for experimentation purposes. You can use GPUs like ASUS DUAL Radeon RX 480 8GB OC, ASRock Radeon RX 5700, MSI GeForce GTX 1660 Ventus XS OC, and XT Phantom Gaming D to mine Monero. You can make $11 a month mining Monero using a GPU with a current hash rate of 10MHz. You get around 4.99 XMR as a mining reward, and the transaction fee shared by validators is 0.06573 XMR per block. The verification time of a block is 2 minutes. There are numerous pools you can connect to. These include ones in which you can partake in profit-switching when you're mining Monero or merge mining. If you wish to mine solo, you will end up investing large sums of money in GPU mining hardware.

Ravencoin

Ravencoin is considered among the most rewarding altcoins to mine. Numerous platforms use it to represent several types of assets, including shares, virtual goods, and gold. Those who wish to mine this coin should opt for NVIDIA GPUs, especially ones from the RTX series. Ravencoin can also be mined using a CPU. Using a GPU, you can make a daily profit of $4.40 at 70 MH/s. The reward for mining is 5000 RVNs per block.

Ethereum Classic

Ethereum Classic uses the Ethash algorithm tweak known as the Thanos or EtcHash upgrade. The Jasminer X4 is named the top Ethereum Classic mining machine by the F2pool mining pool. You can use the machine to make $76.01 of daily profit at a 2,500 mH/z hash rate. The JASMINER X4 BRICK is among other possible machines you can use.

Dogecoin

Dogecoin has witnessed a dramatic rise over the years, especially during 2021. It grants a mining reward of 10,000 DOGE per block, making it a very appealing target for crypto miners, especially GPU users. Dogecoin is a meme coin built on the Scrypt algorithm. This algorithm enables the merged mining of coins. For example, you can easily merge mine Dogecoin with Litecoin on your GPU without impacting the performance of your machine. This is why it is among the top coins to mine using a GPU. The RTX 3090 Ultra Gaming is the best GPU when it comes to mining Dogecoin. However, RTX 2070, RX 580 GTS, AMD Radeon RX 5700XT, RTX 2080 Ti, and the GeForce GTX 1080 Ti are great too. At a 9,500 MH/s mining hash rate, you can make a profit of $49.99 per day.

Zcash

Zcash, which is also regarded as a great coin to mine nowadays, uses the Equihash algorithm. This algorithm is a slightly modified version of the proof-of-work algorithm. It is better suited for GPU mining than it is for ASIC mining. You can use NVIDIA's GTX 1080, GTX 1070Ti, AMD Vega 56/64, GTX 1070, and Nvidia GTX 1070. The lucrativeness of each differs from one GPU to the other. You can make a daily profit of $6.87 at a 135,000 H/s hash rate.

The Coins We're Mining

This book mainly focuses on mining Bitcoin, Ethereum (before it switches to proof-of-stake consensus protocol), Dogecoin, Litecoin, Zcash, and Monero, and here's why:

Bitcoin

Bitcoin is currently the leading cryptocurrency when it comes to its market capitalization. While we encourage mining it, it isn't the number one ranked coin when it comes to generating profits. This is because there are numerous ASIC mining rigs already on the network. For those who don't have millions to spare to invest in specialized hardware, mining Bitcoin would not be worth much. Regardless, you may be surprised to learn that there is a great reason to mine Bitcoin, which is increasing decentralization on the network. Numerous Bitcoin enthusiasts suggest that no other cryptocurrency offers the same level of censorship-resistance and immutability a decentralized currency needs as Bitcoin does. This is why they believe that partaking in securing the number one cryptocurrency is worth the cost of setting up a small Bitcoin mining rig. This means that Bitcoin mining isn't for you if you're seeking nothing but profits.

Ethereum

If you're seeking a coin with great long-term potential, then Ethereum is for you. Many industry experts believe that it can overtake Bitcoin, becoming the most prized asset in the world of cryptocurrency. However, it is worth mentioning that we recommend mining Ethereum before it officially adopts the proof-of-stake consensus protocol.

In the long run, Ethereum is a promising project because its network enables the creation of applications on top of it (we will be exploring the Ethereum use cases in more depth). There was a buzz surrounding the possibility of creating decentralized home-sharing and ride-hailing applications platforms on the Ethereum network. If these platforms share the success of their centralized counterparts, the value of the cryptocurrency will undoubtedly sky-rocket.

There is the talk of decentralized home-sharing apps like Airbnb or the equivalent of ride-sharing platforms like Uber being created on the Ethereum network. If one of these applications proves as successful as their centralized equivalents, the value of Ether tokens will shoot up. Many leading companies are also very interested in Ethereum and are experimenting with blockchain applications backed by the currency.

Dogecoin

Dogecoin first started out as a meme cryptocurrency. However, it has visibly come a very long way since then. Although its creators initially intended for the cryptocurrency to be a ridiculous parody project, the asset boasts a beaming $32 billion market capitalization. Not to mention that it has gained traction all across the globe. The coin's value has risen dramatically over the first half of 2021. This phenomenon is because it has been promoted by Elon Musk, the CEO of Tesla, and thus caught the eye of the internet. This has renewed the interest in Dogecoin mining, spiking mining profitability to a novel six-year high. Even though it is incredibly popular, the mining of Dogecoin is still a lot less competitive than mining Bitcoin. You can also quickly discover new blocks and receive higher rewards than you would with Bitcoin.

Litecoin

A former software engineer at Google named Charlie Lee declared the creation of Litecon in October 2011. The new cryptocurrency was announced as a tweaked clone of Bitcoin, designed for more effective scaling. A bit over 7 years later, Litecoin showed the resilience and staying power other altcoins didn't. The average transaction fees of the cryptocurrency are significantly lower than Bitcoin. The coin's algorithm is also built on mining a new block every 2.5 minutes, four times quicker than Bitcoin.

Zcash

Zcash is a privacy-driven cryptocurrency. As we mentioned above, it is ASIC-resistant, which is why it is a very popular choice among miners. This feature makes it highly profitable even though it uses cheaper GPU chips.

Monero

Monero is another privacy coin with real use cases in the world. Many people already use Monero to buy and sell things on dark web marketplaces, which is why some people are reluctant to mine it. The privacy features of the coin make it really challenging to crack down on its use. The best thing about mining this altcoin is that the process can be very profitable regardless of whether you use GPUs or CPUs. This is primarily because it uses a unique hashing algorithm known as CryptoNote. Setting up a mining rig for Monero is also very easy, making it a perfect choice for beginners.

Ethereum's Use Cases

Decentralized Finance - Defi

Decentralized finance refers to financial products and services that anyone who uses Ethereum has access to. This means there are no authorities to block or deny payments and access, and the markets are always available. This way, you aren't limited by certain trading hours, time zones, and the denial of centralized and financial services. Defi allows you full control over your money. Additionally, you can transfer funds in a few minutes, borrow funds at your own terms (with/ without collateral), purchase insurance, trade tokens, etc.

Non-Fungible Tokens - NFTs

NFTs are unique items that aren't interchangeable. They allow you to attach value to any media file in terms of digital currency. NFTs are secured on the Ethereum blockchain and are only allowed one owner at a time. These tokens are compatible with everything built on the Ethereum platform.

Decentralized Autonomous Organizations - DAOs

DAOs are collectively owned and controlled by their participants. They are internet-based with built-in treasuries and work based on smart contracts. These organizations can't be accessed if their members don't grant that permission. DAOs make use of voting and proposals for decision-making purposes to ensure fairness. There is transparency regarding activities and codes, and the operations are democratic.

Key Takeaways

- You need to consider numerous things when selecting a coin to mine, including profitability, long-term potential, and decentralization on the network.
- While PoS is more eco-friendly, it is inferior to PoW in terms of security, fault tolerance, fork choice, social scalability, a proxy for value, and the accumulation of work.
- The most commonly mined coins include Bitcoin, Monero, Ravencoin, Ethereum Classic, Dogecoin, and Zcash.
- This book mainly focuses on mining Bitcoin, Ethereum, Dogecoin, Litecoin, Zcash, and Monero due to their added benefits and PoW operations.
- Ethereum's use cases include defi, NFTs, and DAOs.

Read through the following chapter to find out more about mining strategies.

3

Mining Strategies

As you were reading the previous chapter, you may have picked up on the fact that there are numerous ways to mine cryptocurrencies, including the use of GPUs or ASICs. This chapter will explain the differences between Bitcoin mining and Ethereum mining. We will explore the different ways to mine cryptocurrencies so you can choose the best one for your needs.

Bitcoin vs. Ethereum

Bitcoin and Ethereum are the two most popular digital tokens. They are the largest cryptocurrencies in terms of market capitalization. Surely, both cryptocurrencies share similar features. For instance, they are both decentralized, are traded through online exchanges, and use the blockchain or distributed ledger technology. However, because the two cryptocurrencies were built to fulfill different purposes, there are significant differences between Bitcoin and Ethereum mining. At first glance, it can be very hard to pick up on these details. But as you read on, you will come to see the prominent contrast between them.

To understand their differences, we must first look into why these cryptocurrencies were established.

The Basics of Bitcoin

Bitcoin was created in January 2009 by Satoshi Nakamoto. While the idea of a decentralized, online currency sounded very appealing, naturally, the public was very skeptical. Bitcoins aren't tangible and are only signified by balances added to a cryptographically secured public ledger. Not many people know that Bitcoin wasn't the first-ever decentralized digital currency. It came to be known as the predecessor of all cryptocurrencies because it was and continues to be the most successful. As the years passed, most people, including governments, authorities, and regulators, have started to accept the idea of a digital, decentralized currency. Even though cryptocurrencies aren't still officially recognized as a means of payment and don't have a formal store value, these tokens still manage to carve out their own niche. The fact they managed to overcome social debates and scrutiny and find a way to fit into the current financial system just proves their promising future.

The Basics of Ethereum

Established in July 2015, Ethereum capitalized on the fact that you can use Blockchain technology to enable digital currencies and create applications. Ethereum came to be known as the best established and largest open-ended decentralized software platform. Ethereum allows the deployment of smart contracts and enables the building and running of decentralized applications without any third-party interference, fraud, downtime, or control. It even utilizes its own unique programming language. This allows developers to create and operate distributed applications.

There is a vast range of prospective Ethereum applications powered by ether, Ethereum's native cryptographic token. The presale for ether was launched in 2014, which surprisingly gained huge traction. Ether is mainly used for two purposes. You can trade it like other cryptocurrencies on an online crypto exchange or use it to run applications on the Ethereum network.

Main Differences

Even though both cryptocurrencies are created on the concepts of cryptography and distributed ledgers, both of them have numerous technical differences. For instance, the data associated with the transactions on the Bitcoin network are to keep notes, while the transactions on the Ethereum network can include executable code. Block time and the algorithms they use are also other differences. While Ethereum runs on Ethash, Bitcoin runs on SHA-256.

As you know, Bitcoin and Ethereum both currently use a proof-of-work protocol. However, Ethereum is expected to move to the proof-of-stake mechanisms this year as part of its Eth2 upgrade. The main difference between Bitcoin and Ethereum is that they're built for different reasons. While Bitcoin was primarily created to serve as an alternate currency to fiat money, Ethereum was created as a platform to facilitate immutable and programmatic contracts and applications through the use of its own currency. This means that even though ETH is a digital currency like BTC, its main purpose is to monetize and enable the Ethereum decentralized application (dApp) platform and smart contracts to operate.

Ethereum's popularity has pushed it to compete with other currencies on the crypto market. However, it was initially intended to support the Bitcoin network and serve as an alternate use case for blockchain technology.

Bitcoin Mining vs. Ethereum Mining

Bitcoin Mining

As we explained in the previous chapter, a miner needs to solve a mathematical equation to add the blocks to the blockchain. Each block utilizes a hash code derived from the block that precedes it to time stamp it. It takes 10 minutes to add blocks to the blockchain. The miners compete against each other to solve the equation, whose answer is supposed to start with four zeros. A miner must have sufficient electricity and computer processing power to do that. The first one to figure out the answer gets rewarded with 12 BTC.

The blockchain miners work together to ensure that the longest chain of transactions is the accurate one. The blockchain remains valid as long as 51% of the miners, or nodes, are honest. The process of validating the blockchain is known as consensus.

Bitcoin Unspent Transaction Output Scheme

Bitcoin uses the UTXO scheme, which is the unspent transaction output scheme, to prevent double-spending on the network and keep track of the database. Users don't transfer Bitcoin as they complete their transactions in this protocol. What they do is that they transfer the digitally signed hash of the previous block along with the public key of the new owner.

Intrinsically, Bitcoin owners don't necessarily hold Bitcoin. Instead, the owners maintain the output to a certain number of tokens that can be signed over to a new user, which transfers the control over the tokens to them in the Bitcoin UTXO blockchain protocol. This can be summed up in the three rules of the protocol:

1. The sum of inputs of each transaction must be larger than the sum of its inputs.
2. All referenced inputs have to be accurate and valid. They must not show as spent.
3. Each input should have a signature that refers to the input's owner.

According to these rules, each Bitcoin transaction must include both inputs and outputs to be valid and complete. The only exception is that as a new Bitcoin is being created in the mining process, there will be outputs and no inputs. This process is known as the Coinbase transaction.

Bitcoin Mining Difficulty

The mining difficulty of Bitcoin has increased greatly over the past two years. This change happened as a result of increasing hash power on the network. As we explained in the previous chapter, this change in difficulty is necessary to adjust to the added hash power and ensure that the block time doesn't fall below 10 minutes.

The great rise in Bitcoin's network hash power started to take place in 2015 upon the launch of Bitmain's Antminer line.

Antminer used unique application-specific integrated chips known as ASIC. These were x1000 better at finishing Bitcoin's algorithm SHA-256. These improvements in hardware made it harder and more expensive to meet the requirements of mining Bitcoin. If you want to be competitive in the current Bitcoin mining environment, you will need to use an ASIC miner and join a mining pool. Mining pools support your efforts since they combine your computing power with that of the entire pool. The rewards you receive will depend on your contribution level.

Ethereum Mining

Aside from the differences we mentioned above, Ethereum utilizes the Solidity programming language, which facilitates smart contract integration. These contracts ease token creation using ERC-721 and ERC-20 protocols. ERC-20 has become the chief token creation protocol in the crypto scene. Meanwhile, the ERC-721 got adopted again with the rise of the tokenization of both physical and digital assets. The primary difference is that ERC-20 tokens are fungible, while ERC-721 tokens aren't.

In essence, the main operations of the Ethereum mining process are just like Bitcoin's, in the sense that miners compete against each other to solve mathematical equations. The node that succeeds receives an award of 3.5 ETH. However, the Ethereum block time is much faster. A new block is added to the blockchain every 14 to 16 seconds.

Ethereum Account-Based Protocol

Ethereum uses a less complex approach to prevent double-spending. It tracks transactions in a way that is similar to traditional bank accounts. Ethereum owners directly send their tokens and not just digitally signed hash inputs, unlike Bitcoin. This means that each transaction directly affects each Ethereum account in terms of the flow of information and value transfers. Account-based protocols can only be achieved with centralization. The Ethereum team reviews your request to ensure that you have the token in your wallet first before you can send a transaction. This process enables you to refund, reverse, or void transactions whenever you wish.

Ethereum Mining Difficulty

While the Ethereum platform witnessed an increase in the hash rate since 2016, the numbers aren't nearly as close to Bitcoin's. The Ethereum mining scene isn't as competitive as Bitcoin's, which is why you can still use GPUs for mining. Even though GPUs are a lot more powerful than CPUs (central processing units), they still fall significantly short of the capabilities and features of ASIC miners.

When compared to ASIC miners, it's easy to point out the pros and cons of GPU miners. For instance, you can mine several cryptocurrencies using GPUs, regardless of the hash algorithms they use. This flexibility and range are indispensable for many miners and their strategies. Because they lack many of the performance capabilities of the ASIC mining rigs, GPU miners are a lot more affordable. While you only need one power supply to power an ASIC mining rig, GPUs come in many devices.

Changes: What to Expect?

While we recommend mining cryptocurrency that uses the proof-of-work consensus protocol for the many reasons we covered in the previous chapter, PoS relieves miners from the need for great amounts of computing power and expensive hardware. Crypto owners stake their coins in their wallets on the blockchain and get rewarded based on the number of coins they have.

Ethereum's decision to switch to a PoS protocol helps diminish the issue of centralization on the blockchain. There are currently five mining pools that hold dominion over the mining sectors of Ethereum. Three of them alone, namely f2pool_2, ethfans.org, and Ethermine, are responsible for 85% of the hash rate of the Ethereum network.

These changes will ultimately change how Ethereum miners get rewarded for their efforts. Until the transition to PoS is finalized, the developers of Ethereum aim to build a hybrid system. This would allow miners to ease into the transition as the network slowly adopts these changes.

Profitability: Bitcoin vs. Ethereum Mining

It would be very hard to make solid comparisons between the profitability of Bitcoin and that of Ethereum because there are numerous factors to consider. You will need substantial investment to begin your mining operations either way. You should also keep in mind that Bitcoin is a lot scarcer than Ethereum at this point. However, this scarcity could mean that Bitcoin holders will witness incredible gains in the future. In retrospect, Ethereum offers special features in the cryptocurrency scene. Not many people realize that ERC-20 and ERC-712, both its protocols, serve as the backbone of most of the tokens you can get ahold of in the crypto marketplace. Since other tokens depend on Ethereum so much, this created the possibility of having Ethereum overtake Bitcoin in terms of total market capitalization in the next few years.

Now that you are aware of the main differences between Bitcoin and Ethereum, we will start exploring the different mining strategies and options you have.

Cryptocurrency Mining Strategies and Options

There are several ways in which you can mine cryptocurrency. We will now cover the most popular ones, starting with the easiest method: cloud mining.

Cloud Mining

Cloud mining is the most popular and easiest way to mine cryptocurrency. All you need to do is pay someone, typically a large, specialized corporation, a certain amount of money to rent out a rig. All the earnings made by the rig go to your cryptocurrency wallet for the agreed renting period. These companies typically have large mining facilities and are very experienced when it comes to crypto mining. This is ideal for those who aren't financially capable of buying a rig or simply those who don't wish to own one.

Cloud mining comes with two options: free and paid. Although the free option sounds very appealing, it has its disadvantages, such as slow mining speeds. If you use the paid option, you can search for an online cloud mining host and browse through the plans they offer. After you subscribe to your desired plan, you enter your crypto wallet address. The standard plans can cost anywhere between $500 and $5000.

CPU Mining

CPU mining is not as popular or as feasible as it was before. This is primarily because it's incredibly slow to work with. Miners can go months without catching a glimpse of revenue. You may also end up spending much more than you make in terms of cooling and electricity. However, some people resort to that option simply because any desktop computer can get this process done. All you need is your device and a few programs. Avoid using your laptop if you wish to try it out because it will overheat very quickly.

GPU Mining

GPU mining is the most popular crypto mining method. Even the cloud mining option we mentioned above involves the use of GPUs. This method is very efficient and relatively affordable. While the rig setup is costly, it isn't expensive in terms of hash speed and the overall workforce. GPU miners use graphic cards to mine coins. A standard rig comprises around 2 to 8 graphics cards, processor, cooling, motherboard, and rig frame. While creating a GPU rig is a hefty investment of around $3000, you can pay it off much faster than you would with a CPU miner.

ASIC Mining

Application-Specific Integrated Circuits, more commonly known as ASICs, are specially designed for crypto mining. They are incredibly popular and valued because they generate great amounts of cryptocurrency in comparison to CPU and GPU miners. Unfortunately, because these devices are so popular, they make it extremely hard for miners who don't own them to keep up with hash speeds and, of course, make earnings. These machines are incredibly expensive, retailing for around $5500.

Best Crypto Mining Method

The best crypto mining method for your needs depends on the amount of money you are willing to spend upfront. People gravitate toward GPU mining and cloud mining. CPU mining should be avoided, and ASIC mining is very expensive and highly unpredictable due to the surrounding controversy. If you're willing to take the risk, ASIC miners are the way to go, but if you want to build your own rig, then go for GPUs.

Key Takeaways

- Bitcoin was fundamentally created as an alternative for fiat currency, while Ethereum aims to be a platform that facilitates immutable and programmatic contracts and applications through the use of ETH.
- Bitcoin uses the UTXO scheme, while Ethereum uses a less complex account-based approach to prevent double-spending.
- The Ethereum mining scene isn't as competitive as Bitcoin's. This is why you won't stand a chance if you're not using ASICs to mine Bitcoins but can use GPUs to mine Ethereum.
- Joining a mining pool can be of great help and even crucial at times.
- The main mining strategies include cloud mining, CPU mining, GPU Mining, and ASICs mining. Your choice comes down to your budget, needs, and whether you wish to own a rig or even intend to mine using one.

Read on to find out more about how to mine with NiceHash.

4

Mining with NiceHash

Another mining strategy would be to start mining with NiceHash. In this part of the chapter, we will be exploring what NiceHash is, how it works, and why you should consider using it. We'll also explain how you can mine with your gaming computer using NiceHash and how you can set up your GPU with the platform.

What Is NiceHash?

NiceHash is the crypto marketplace's largest hash power. It aims to connect miners or sellers with those who wish to buy hash power. Hash power refers to the power your hardware needs to run and solve the PoW hashing algorithms of various cryptocurrencies. NiceHash is not like any other platform because it doesn't offer any mining equipment or cloud mining option but only connects end-users to each other.

How It Works

This platform allows buyers to partake in an open marketplace. There, they can browse through various cryptocurrencies and select the one they wish to mine and the pool on which they would like to mine. The buyers can also set the price they want to pay and place their orders. The buyers receive the cryptocurrency from the pool as soon as the miners with NiceHash Miner Legacy running on their machines complete their orders. This way, buyers will not need to acquire expensive mining hardware or get involved in complicated mining operations themselves.

Miners, who are sellers in that case, can run the NiceHash miner software or connect your mining rig (regular PC, GPU, ASIC) to NiceHash and the buyer's order. The pool the buyer selects receives the buyer's hashing power, and for each valid share submitted, they get rewarded in Bitcoins. The Bitcoin payment depends on the price, which is determined by the current weighted average. It is refreshed each minute for accuracy. These are things that can be done automatically. You don't need any complex technical knowledge.

In short, NiceHash is not a mining pool. This platform allows miners to sell hashing power to the buyers who redirect that power to the pool.

Why You Should Mine with NiceHash

Many miners prefer using NiceHash for mining over directly mining to a pool because of the various advantages it offers. These include:

A Low Payout Threshold

NiceHash's internal accounting systems enable the transfer of Bitcoins, in small amounts, from the buyers to the miners. 0.00001 BTC is the minimum payout threshold, which is an amount that can be achieved in just a few hours if you're using an average mining rig. Mining pools, however, have a much higher payout threshold of at least 0.005 BTC, which would take a couple of weeks to achieve if you're using one GPU or a single mining rig.

Payouts

Blockchain transactions aren't issued for order payment, mining, and other coin movements across the NiceHash systems. This makes it possible for miners to make payouts once every four hours as long as they reach the minimum 0.00001 BTC payment. If you join a mining pool, you'll probably be able to make payouts once a day if you reach the minimum payout threshold. How frequently you can initiate a payout is determined by the time it takes you to reach the minimum threshold. For some people, this can take days or weeks.

Those who buy hash power can use Bitcoin as a form of payment for hashing power, which is why all miners get paid in BTC. The platform also supports EUR withdrawals, allowing you to transfer your earnings to your bank account. NiceHash allows you to withdraw or trade your earnings whenever you want, which is a great option when the transaction fees are too high.

Tax Reporting

This is why NiceHash is an ideal option for those who prefer Bitcoin payments. The platform offers a document of all your past activity, including your mining earnings, which helps with tax reporting.

Other benefits include a pay-per-share reward system, ease of use, auto-updates, profit switching, security, NiceHash Exchange, human support, and access to the largest and smartest crypto communities.

Mining Using NiceHash on Your Gaming PC

Any GTX graphics card with Pascal architecture can be used to mine cryptocurrency. This means you can use your gaming PC, but you have to be very mindful of the electricity costs. Since you probably won't be mining all day long every single day, you should consider using a mining pool or a service like NiceHash that allows you to get in and out when you aren't using your PC. You need to ensure you have enough cooling and keep in mind that the fans can get very loud if they're running at 100% efficiency. Many people think that mining can wear down the components of your PC. However, it's the heat that kills them.

1. Prepare Your Gaming PC for Mining

To begin, you will set up an account on the NiceHash website and then download the mining software. Run it and type in your NiceHash address. Then, click on the large play button.

2. Create a Bitcoin Wallet

As you start to build up cryptocurrency from the buyers on NiceHash, you should decide where you wish to store it. Even though you can keep it in your NiceHash wallet, we advise storing it in a separate specialized crypto wallet. Once you've reached the minimum payout threshold, you can transfer your money from NiceHash to your wallet. Many people prefer to use a physical wallet, an offline device that stores all your details regarding cryptocurrency, for extra security.

3. Find a Bitcoin Mining Pool

After you have your wallet set up, you need to consider joining a Bitcoin mining pool. Keep in mind that even those who use ASIC miners can find it hard to mine in today's competitive market. It would be very hard to compete against huge mining farms worldwide. To navigate through these limitations, your only option is to join a mining pool. You need to conduct thorough research to determine which mining pool to join. Sometimes, you may have to pay a fee to join a mining pool, which you need to keep in mind. After that, you should create an account and observe your earnings as they flow in.

It is worth saying that there is a large mining pool concentration in China. It is the highest in the world, comprising about 20 huge mining pools. If you break down the percentage of hash power a pool controls and the headquarters of that pool, it is around 65% of the network's hash rate.

4. Find a Crypto Mining Software

After you've joined a mining pool and set up your wallet, it's time to download crypto mining software on your gaming PC. Some mining pools come with their own software. If yours doesn't have one, there are many other options you should look into. The client serves as a tie between your PC and the Bitcoin blockchain. The crypto mining software also keeps track of statistics, such as the temperature of your PC and your mining rate. BTCMine,

BFGMiner, Ethminer, and CGMiner are a few crypto mining software you should look into.

5. Start Mining
Now that you have everything ready, you can start mining.

6. Optimize Your Gaming PC for Crypto Mining
Technically speaking, you can use NiceHash and have it run for years. However, it would be better to optimize it to make the best use of your GPU without using too much electricity. You can lower your costs without affecting your efficiency or performance, and in turn, you can earn more profit. You can use the tool MSI Afterburner that allows you to alter your clock speed GPU power, along with other rates.

To reduce your GPU power consumption, you can run the MSI Afterburner and set the power limit to 80%. Then, press the apply button and begin mining on NiceHash. Keep track of the hash rate in MH/s. You can find it in the miner command line window. Set the power limit in Afterburner to a lower 5%. Press the Apply button once more and keep track of your hash rate once more 10 minutes later. Repeat the previous 3 steps until your hash rate drops or you reach the allowed minimum power limit.

Set Up Your GPU with NiceHash

If you have your mining rig all set up with your GPUs installed, it's time to start mining. One way to do that is by using NiceHash to optimize your rig fully in under one hour. Here's how you can set up your GPU with NiceHash:

1. Install Windows

The first step is to install Windows 10 x64, either the Home or Pro version. The version doesn't matter as long as it's the 64-bit and not x86. Make sure to unplug all but one of your GPUs. Having just one GPU up and running makes it a lot easier to diagnose and troubleshoot issues. The BIOS settings you use are not that important. The most important thing is that you can boot the installation drive and install Windows 10.

2. Install NVIDIA Drivers

Installing the non-DCH version of the NVIDIA drivers is a very important step. Use Advanced Driver Search in the NVIDIA driver download web page to find them. It's worth mentioning that recent DCH drivers are very faulty when it comes to memory leaks. This is why they aren't recommended for mining purposes. After the installation is complete, make sure that the process is successful. Use GPU-Z to verify that.

If the installation fails, you will likely find that the majority of the checkboxes aren't checked. If almost or all are checked, then the installation process was successful. You'll also be able to tell the driver version and if your driver is non-DCH or DCH through GPU-Z.

3. Install NiceHash QuickMiner

Download and install the latest NiceHash QuickMiner release. Beware that you may experience some issues with Windows Defender. All you need to do is click on allow NiceHashQuickMiner.exe and excavator.exe. Also, configure your mining address to link your NiceHash account with your rig. Name your rig, and then make sure your error handling mechanism is set to reboot the rig. You shouldn't enable start with Windows just yet. The next step is to find out if your rig is visible in Rig Manager and that you can control it. Change

OPTIMIZE or start or stop it to test it out. Once you ensure that everything is working, you need to reboot your rig into BIOS.

4. BIOS Settings

If you are using more than 3 GPUs, and/or if at least one GPU is connected using USB-risers, you need to configure these settings:

- Above 4G decoding should be set to enabled. If your motherboard provides a number of bits, make sure to set it at 40 or 41. Avoid going over 41 because a lot of devices could have problems.
- Find the settings for the PCIe link. You should configure all the slots that use the USB-riser to PCIe Gen1 or PCIe Gen2. While the higher the Gen, the higher the speed, USB risers are not created with high speed in mind. This means it rarely works with Gen 3 and can never work with Gen 4. Gen 1 can also sometimes have compatibility problems, so stick to Gen 2.
- Set the BIOS setting to UEFI boot only and ensure that CSM or legacy is disabled. This way, you will face the least issues possible during the GPU detection process.
- If you have an integrated GPU in your CPU or motherboard, enable it and set it as the primary GPU. Then, plug HDMI/DP or monitor cable into the motherboard. Rendering displays can decrease the hash rate, so make sure to use integrated GPU if you can.
- When power loss occurs, turn on the action, so your rig automatically turns on if your device loses power.
-

If you follow these configurations, you should be able to use up to 13 GPUs in your rig without encountering any problems.

5. Reconnect All Hardware or GPUs
After you configure your BIOS setting, shut everything down and connect all your GPUs again. The power should be distributed well.

6. Starting Windows with All GPUs
Give your rig time to install all the GPUs it just detected. This can take around 15 to 20 minutes, and your screen may flicker in the process. Check Device Manager to verify the number of display adapters detected. They should equal the number of GPUs you have, including integrated ones. Use GPU-Z again to check if the installation of the drivers was completed successfully.

7. Start QuickMiner and Optimize for Mining
Go to the Rig Manager in QuickMiner. All devices should be set to Lite Optimization and left running for 10 minutes. If the Excavator doesn't crash as you wait, you don't have any problems. Set all your devices to the Optimize profile you want. They are typically set at Efficient. Move to a lower profile and reboot your rig if anything crashes. Once you're good to go. Enable the setting to start QuickMiner with Windows.

Key Takeaways

- NiceHash is another mining strategy that serves as the crypto marketplace's largest hash power.
- NiceHash connects miners, or sellers, with those who wish to buy hash power, allowing buyers to partake in an open marketplace.
- NiceHash is more advantageous than directly joining a mining pool because it has a lower payout threshold,

offers quicker payouts, helps with tax reporting, offers human support, and is easy to use.

Read on to find out more about Compass Mining.

5

Using Compass Mining

Compass Mining is the perfect tool for you if you don't want to set up your own mining rig. We'll explore Compass Mining, why you should consider using it, and how you can use it.

What Is Compass Mining?

Like NiceHash, Compass Mining serves as an intermediary and a marketplace. It connects people with hosting facilities and mining hardware. It also connects people with miners, those who wish to purchase hosting space, or both. Compass Mining creates deals with facilities that own extra capacity and space to host mining equipment. If you visit their facilities page, you will find a wide array of the facilities they have partnered up with.

While most of these facilities are located in Canada and the United States, others are located in other countries. Every facility creates a listing that includes its hosting price and states if it uses a renewable or non-renewable energy source. Most of the facilities have a hosting price of $0.060 to $0.065 per kWh. This fee includes the slot on the rack inside the facility, electricity consumption, which makes up the bulk of the price you pay, and a charge for the technician's time and effort on setting up and monitoring your mining equipment in the facility. It's worth mentioning that the total price offered by Compass Mining is likely less than half the price you pay for electricity if you set up a rig at home. This is because the hosting facilities get commercial rates. They also set up their rigs in cheap areas with abundant electrical resources. You should also know that Compass Mining isn't an example of cloud mining. Even though you don't have to set up your mining rig at home, you will have full ownership over your hardware if you use Compass. You also have flexibility when moving machines from one facility to the other, swapping mining pools, or even selling your rig to other miners.

You can also find an ASIC collection for sale at Compass. If you check, you will find that the selection of rigs alternate over time. This is primarily due to the fluctuations in demand. ASIC prices are inclined to rapid appreciation when the prices of Bitcoin appreciate, according to Zack Voell, the Content Director at Compass. However, when the price of Bitcoin declines, ASICs' prices depreciate at a slow pace. This is because they get "sticky" when they're running and mining Bitcoin.

For instance, during the first half of 2021, the market experienced a very sharp shortage of ASICs. The price of Bitcoin was steadily increasing, which triggered more demand for ASICs. However, the producers couldn't keep up with this demand, which is why all available ASICs became incredibly valuable. When Bitcoin fell to a more stable price, the price of ASICs decreased and became easier to get ahold of. Now, the congestion lies within hosting facilities. China continues to produce hundreds of thousands of ASIC mining machines, new hosting facilities are being built in North America alongside other regions, and Compass still offers space at specific contracted facilities. According to the company's CEO, Compass is currently expanding its capacity.

How Does It Work?

The company gets a wide array of customers and miners. The great thing about Compass is that it can be used as an all-encompassing solution you can use to embark on your mining journey. You can purchase an ASIC miner through compass and host it at one of the facilities they're contracted with. This facility will hook up your mining machinery for you. Then, you can select the mining pool you wish to join and provide Compass a public Bitcoin address so they can send you your earnings.

Purchasing the ASICs and finding a facility plan will only take you a few minutes. You'll have everything ready and running a few weeks after that. Once they set up your ring, you will contact the mining department to discuss linking your connection to the mining pool you selected and receiving your earnings to the address you provided. This will take you another few minutes. After that, you will be able to start mining. You can log into your mining pool account to check up on your miners' updates and states. You can also make sure that your earnings are delivered to your address.

Why You Should Mine with Compass Mining

Compass Mining is a Bitcoin-driven institute. It aims to support the growth of the decentralized hash rate. Its mission is also to strengthen the security of the network. They intend to do so by providing people the opportunity to explore and learn about, and of course, mine Bitcoin.

Compass Mining is created to eliminate the unnecessary inconveniences of having your own mining rig. You don't need to worry about your device overheating, setting up your rig, designating an area for it, and maintaining it over time. Compass Mining offers an all-inclusive mining experience that makes the process easy and hassle-free. You can put your worries away and enjoy the mining process. Another great thing about Compass Mining is that it prioritizes its miners. It provides impeccable 24/7 top-tier service and customer support. Central to the Compass Mining company is the idea that centralization is crucial to maintain a strong, secure, and safe network. This is why they make sure that miners can mine in different parts of the world, as this will help spread the hash rate.

How to Mine with Compass Mining

Not many people are aware they can mine Bitcoin without setting up a rig at home. Besides the cloud mining option, Compass Mining provides an out-of-home hosting experience. If you're considering using this company's services, you can follow this simple five-step procedure. You can also check out the

Compass Mining education library if you wish to learn more about the process or the crypto industry in general.

1. Visit the Website: Compassmining.io
Visit their website compassmining.io and click on the hardware window on the navigation bar to get started.

2. Select an ASIC
You will find a wide array of ASIC mining machines on the hardware page. Browse through to compare prices and features. You can either look the devices up or contact the Compass team for support and information. You can also connect with communities of more experienced miners online if you need a second opinion.

3. Choose a Hosting Facility
On the navigation bar, click on Facilities to browse through the several hosting facilities available. Find a region you want your machine to operate in. You will likely find available spots at mining farms across the globe. You will always know the exact place at which your machine is hashing in, and you will have the freedom to move it around.

4. Join a Mining Pool
Now that you have your ASICs installed at your desired facility, the Compass team will contact you to connect your machine to the mining pool of your choice. You may want to check with the company in case there are any guidelines regarding the mining pool selection process.

5. Receive Your BTC Earnings

You have everything set up. Your machines should be hashing and mining Bitcoin at this point. The Company will send out your payouts to the mining pool. Make sure you always have great operations security, or OPSEC, in place, regardless of the amount of Bitcoin you receive and store.

Miner and Hosting Payments

Compass generally accepts two payment methods for the miner and hosting invoices.

Wire Transfers

If you're purchasing a miner by wire, you won't have to pay any additional fees. Make sure to follow the instructions provided by your bank upon filling out the wiring information. The specifications for the instructions may vary from one location to the other, whether inside the US or globally. Make sure you select the right options and keep in mind that the transactions conducted through wire transfer are irreversible. This is why it's important to double-check with your bank before you hit send. The funds sent through wire transfers may take 1 to 2 business days. Once they arrive, you will see your reservation on your dashboard.

If you're paying for hosting through wire transfers, you will pay an additional 1% fee of the total. The maximum charge is typical $5.

Cryptocurrency

The other payment method you can use is cryptocurrency. You don't need to pay an additional fee if you're purchasing a miner or paying for hosting using Bitcoin from Compass.

Key Takeaways

- You can also use Compass Mining if you don't wish to mine at home.
- Compass isn't a cloud mining company because you get to have ownership and control over your mining rig when you use it.

If you want to set up a rig yourself, read the following chapter to know-how.

6

Setting Up Your Rig

"The more you dig deeper into crypto, the more you will discover you know little about so many things in life. Keep learning and never stop!" - Olawale Daniel

For those who don't know, cryptocurrency mining is the process of solving mathematical equations to discover blocks on the blockchain. This gives the miner who discovers a block a specific amount of cryptocurrency. A successful solution eventually gets added to the blockchain.

YouTube is full of videos on how to set up your rig, but most of them only cover the basics. This chapter will take a look at the components you need to assemble your rig, give some insights into the software required to mine cryptocurrency, and then show you how to assemble your rig.

Introduction to Cryptocurrency Mining

Cryptocurrencies such as Bitcoin, Litecoin, and Ethereum are decentralized peer-to-peer currencies that need to be mined to be created. Mining is an essential process of the crypto-world. To maintain the blockchain, a network of miners that use their computational power help create a new cryptocurrency.

A miner's role is a simple one: find a block, solve its cryptographic riddle with the mining software, and get paid for it.

The algorithm for mining a block is very simple, and it can be broken down into 5 steps:

1. New transactions are broadcast to all the nodes in the network.
2. Miners then collect each new transaction.
3. Miners then group new transactions into blocks, add them to the blockchain, and finally broadcast the completed block to other nodes.
4. The process repeats itself for each new block of transactions found.
5. You are rewarded with a certain amount of Bitcoin for mining a block.

There are also two types of rewards that miners can receive:

1. **Block Rewards** - Since 2015, the miner's reward has been 25 BTC per block found.
2. **Transaction Fees** - Since 2015, the network has allowed miners to include optional transaction fees in their block transactions. These fees are completely voluntary and can be between 0-100% of the total transaction amount. The

miner that includes these fees will get 100% of those fees as an incentive to process your transactions on their mining rig.

Prerequisites for Mining

Before you begin mining with your GPU, you should follow these steps to ensure that your system is mining efficiently.

1. Update all drivers on your computer, and if you are running Windows 10, then it is recommended that you upgrade to the latest version.
2. If you didn't already, join a mining pool and register an account on their website.
3. Install all of the latest software for your GPUs motherboard, and download ethOS.
4. Install all of the necessary software on Windows 10 by following this guide.
5. Overclock your GPUs so that you get the best hash rates possible.

If you want to build your mining rig for cryptocurrency or Bitcoin, you will need to look at the hardware requirements for your desired level of hash rate and power consumption. The crypto compare mining hardware wiki is a good place to start when deciding how to build your mining rig, and it provides a comprehensive list of GPU hash rates and power consumption depending on what software you will be running.

The Components of Your RIG (Mining Machine)

The hardware you will need for your mining rig is very specific, and most cryptocurrency miners use custom-built rigs to maximize their profit. The following are the main hardware components that make up a good mining rig:

1. **Motherboard** - Many different types of motherboards will work with your mining rig. The most important thing has enough PCI slots to accommodate all of your GPUs.
2. **Processor** - There are 2 main processors used in cryptocurrency mining: AMD and NVIDIA. You want an Intel processor or AMD FX8350 for your motherboard. If you have a PC already, the fastest AMD processor you can find is recommended.
3. **Power Supply Unit (PSU)** - To power your components, you need a PSU that has more than enough wattage to cover all of the components in your rig. Look for an efficient PSU with at least 1200 Watt ratings.
4. **Graphics Cards (GPUs)** - You should use at least a 1060 GPU for NVIDIA. If you have an AMD card, look for the RX580 as it is the best card to mine with.
5. **Hard Drive** - You can either choose a hard drive or just install your OS from an external USB drive. SSDs are faster and more expensive but not needed for mining.
6. **Memory (RAM)** - 8GB of RAM is plenty if you're just starting with mining, and the speed doesn't matter that much. If you want to run on Linux OS, get 16GB of RAM instead.
7. **Power Button**
8. **Case/Rack** - Most people build their mining machines into cases to keep them safe and properly cooled.
9. **Operating System (OS**) - Some people choose to run Windows 10, but you can buy an OS like ethOS made specifically for cryptocurrency mining. You also want to make sure you install the graphics card drivers for

whichever OS you choose before starting your mining rig and before installing the mining software.

Software for Your RIG (Windows)

There are many different types of cryptocurrency mining software available depending upon which currency you want to mine. Here is a list of the most popular ones:

1. **ethOS** - This is an all-in-one Linux OS that mines Ethereum, Zcash, Monero, Pascalcoin, and many other GPU-mineable coins. It is the only mining software that I recommend because it comes with everything you need.
2. **Claymore's Dual Ethereum Miner** - This software is for AMD GPUs and runs on Windows or Linux. Some versions run under ethOS.
3. **Cudo Miner** - This ethOS-based software works best with Nvidia GPUs. It also comes with everything you need to get started mining in one package, including the mining software, overclocking tool, and remote monitoring capabilities.
4. **EWBF Miner** - This software runs on Windows or Linux and is great for Nvidia GPUs.
5. **Nicehash Miner** - This software ran on Windows or Linux and was specifically made to work with their Nicehash mining pool.
6. **EasyMiner** - This mining app comes with basic features on one software, but it can be used alone or integrated into more complex cryptocurrency mining apps.

Building the RIG (Assembly)

You want to build your mining rig inside of a case because it will be cleaner and easier to access all of the cables and connections on your motherboard.

1. First, place your motherboard onto some risers so you have room for all of the PCI slots on the back. Place a block of wood onto the risers to keep your motherboard steady.
2. Put your power supply unit (PSU) inside the case and connect it to all your components with cable extensions. You can buy pre-made extensions or make them yourself if you do not want to go through the hassle.
3. Take all of your GPUs and place them into the PCI slots on the motherboard. When you are done, you should have 4 GPUs in your rig.
4. Connect your monitor to the motherboard using an HDMI cable.
5. Now power on your PSU using its power switch (or remote). You should see all of the fans spinning inside of your rig. If you do not see any activity on the screen, try plugging in a different monitor into the GPU. You can also go into BIOS by pressing F2 or DEL during bootup and check devices for display if one of your GPUs is not recognized by Windows 10.
6. Boot up your OS and install all mining software onto Windows 10.

Testing and Configuring Your RIG (After Assembly)

1. To test whether or not your rig is working properly, you will have to turn it on and wait for a few minutes until either BIOS or OS detects that all 4 GPUs are working properly. You can also check for this information in ethOS by clicking the green "STATUS" button on the left side of the screen.
2. You will then need to set up your mining pool and configure each GPU to work properly with your software.
3. Lastly, you want to configure overclocking settings for both your GPUs and the memory on your motherboard to get the best hash rates out of your mining rig.

Protecting Yourself with a PAPER WALLET

1. If you want to have an extra layer of security, create a paper wallet by using BitAddress or BrainWallet. To create a paper wallet, go to one of these websites and make sure you are connected to the internet with your mining rig turned off (or with a flash drive plugged in).
2. You will then be brought to a screen that contains public and private keys. Save the public key for later use, but do not lose it because you cannot access your cryptocurrency without it. You can then choose a password for your paper wallet, but be careful not to forget it because if you do, you will lose access to it forever.
3. When printing your paper wallet, be sure to check the "Bills" tab and print it on a high-quality setting so that it does not look tampered with or frayed on the edges.
4. Once you have printed your paper wallet, put it in a waterproof and fireproof case (like an old film canister). Then store it somewhere safe, like a safe or a deposit box where only you will be able to access it. Make sure that wherever you decide to store your paper wallet, it is not

near where you store your other valuables because if someone breaks into your house, they might assume that it is worth something and steal it.

Setting Up the Miner: ethOS and Claymore's 9.6

1. Download and install the latest version of ethOS.
2. Follow instructions on how to boot from USB.
3. Plug in all power cables and connect your monitor to one of the GPUs.
4. Boot up your computer and press "e" to edit the command-line options. Type in: disk0 and press Enter and then type in: chainloader +1 and press Enter. Save and exit.
5. After it finishes booting, you will see that two of the GPUs are recognized by the system and that all six of the PCIe ports are 'unoccupied' and have no ethOS assigned to them. Assign ethOS to all six PCIe ports by entering: sudo hotm-swap -a 0,1,2,3.
6. Change overclocking settings in the config file so that you can get a good hash rate for mining Ethos. Look at your GPUs and choose a command-line option based on what type of power supply you have and how many GPUs you will be running. Make sure you change the command-line option to reflect your hardware configuration.
7. If you are using ethOS, then use the web browser on your computer to navigate to your rig's IP address which you can find by typing: sudo ip l and hit Enter.
8. If you want to be able to access your miner with a password, then go to "Log in" and press the "Generate Password" button. Save this password in a safe place

because if you lose it, you will not be able to access your miner again without re-generating it.

The Profit Margin

In an hour, you can mine about 1.5 Ethos on an RX 480 8GB with overclocking settings that give you the maximum hash rate for that particular mining rig. On a computer running Windows 10, you can expect to mine about 1 Ethos every two days, which makes the minimum value of each ethOS $1.35/day or $4.70/week. The price of an RX 480 8GB is between $200-250, so the return on investment for this mining rig will be about one month. Assuming the price of Ethos does not rise or fall, it would take about 3 months to break even in terms of the rig's cost. This particular mining rig is also very easy to upgrade. All of the parts can be swapped out for more powerful ones, which will give your rig a longer lifetime of usefulness.

Getting the Most Out of Your Crypto Mining Rig

To get the most out of your mining rig when you are not using it, there are several options to choose from to ensure that your rig is making the most profit possible. Here are the different things you can do with an off-site mining rig:

1. Hosting on Minerstat (ethOS and BFGMiner Compatible)

The first option is to host your rig on Minerstat and mine Ethos with the EthOS software. You can purchase a $5/mo plan if you want to try this. The advantage of Minerstat is that it has a built-in profit-switching algorithm, which will automatically switch your miner between the most profitable coins without you having to change anything. You can also check your miner's performance by going to the "Dashboard" on the Minerstat website and looking under "My Workers."

2. Mining at NiceHash (ethOS, Linux, Windows)

The next option is to mine other coins at NiceHash, which is great for ethOS users because it can be used with both Linux and Windows. The disadvantage of this option is that the crypto coins you are mining will not automatically go into your wallet like they do when you mine them with EthOS. You also need to consider the fact that NiceHash charges a 3% fee on all the profits you make.

3. Cloud Mining (ethOS and Genoil Compatible Mining)

Another option is cloud mining, which requires you to purchase a certain amount of hash power to use at NiceHash or Minerstat. The benefit of cloud mining is that it will not cost you anything after paying for the hash power, and there is no equipment to maintain. The disadvantage is that if the price of your currency goes up too high, you might end up spending more on the hash power than you will make in return.

4. Monero Mining (ethOS, Linux)

Another option for ethOS users is to mine Monero with XMR-Stak software. The great thing about this option is that it has built-in support for both Linux and Windows operating systems. The only downside is that it does not come with a profit-switching algorithm like Minerstat, so you will have to figure out which coin to mine on your own.

5. Zcash Mining (ethOS, Linux)

Another option for ethOS users is to mine Zcash with EWBF software. The great thing about this option is that it has built-in support for both Linux and Windows operating systems. There are also tests showing that Zcash mining on EWBF gives you a higher hash rate than mining with the Claymore software, which is another reason why this option might be better for you.

You can also buy a GPU-based VPS from Amazon or OVH if you want to mine at Minerstat remotely. You will then need to install either EthOS or Linux into that VPS and connect it to the internet with an ethernet cable.

Mining for cryptocurrency is a fun way to earn extra cash, but it can also be a very frustrating hobby. Keep in mind that you probably will not become a millionaire overnight, but it is a fun way to learn about both world economics and technology in general. This chapter discussed mining, how to get started, and some of the best software you can use for mining.

Key Takeaways

- Mining for cryptocurrency involves using your computer to solve certain equations involved in verifying transactions. The miner who solves them first is rewarded with a specific amount of currency.
- The most popular mining software for computers is ethOS (compatible with both Linux and Windows operating systems). If you would like to try out Minerstat, it is also compatible with ethOS.
- To get started at Minerstat, you will need an account on their website and an email address to receive the account information.
- The best software for mining Monero with an NVIDIA GPU is XMR-Stak, and the best software for mining Zcash

is EWBF. You can also mine Ethereum or other altcoins at Minerstat by using their "Automatic mode" option.

- To mine cryptocurrency, you will need a computer with at least two graphics cards connected to the internet.
- If you are using ethOS for your operations, then you will need to have two USB flash drives plugged into your computer before it can begin mining.
- Like any other computer, you will need a case to hold all the parts together. You can use any type of case you want, but it would be a good idea to use a case with good airflow because your computer will produce a lot of heat while mining.
- The best power supply unit you can use would be a dual PSU or two separate PSUs. You can find cheap power supplies around the internet, but make sure to find out how much electricity a power supply can handle.
- To get started with Minerstat, you will need to sign up for an account on their website. You will receive an email containing your login information, including your username and password.
- Distributing the mining workload is important to keep your rigs from getting overloaded. It can also help prevent errors in your software when it tries to communicate with your GPUs. To do this, you can use a program like Teamviewer to remotely connect to your rig and control it from anywhere in the world.

Mining for cryptocurrency is one of several ways to earn extra cash by using your computer's resources. There are many different options to choose from when it comes to mining software, and each of them has its advantages and disadvantages. While mining will earn you money, it can also be a very frustrating hobby if your equipment goes wrong or the coin you are mining drops in value.

In the next chapter, you will learn the economics of mining.

7

The Economics of Mining

"The best time to plant a tree was twenty years ago. The second best time is now."

- Chinese Proverb

Mining is the process by which transactions are verified and added to a public ledger, known as a blockchain, and also the means through which new Bitcoin (BTC) are released in a process referred to as "Bitcoin mining." One of Satoshi Nakamoto's innovative inventions in the cryptocurrency space was a proof-of-work algorithm that combines cryptography and economics. Its purpose is to secure the Bitcoin network and verify transactions, and as such, it has attracted many computational resources to participate in this process. This is, however, a double-edged sword: it has increased the security of the blockchain immensely, but at the same time, it has also created an ever-increasing resource requirement for mining, which in turn has pushed out the average individual from being able to mine. Consequently, this has perpetuated a high-stakes arms race in mining technology, which created a dynamic and fast-evolving landscape.

Cryptocurrency Mining: Background and Definitions

To better understand the technology in the context of mining, an overview of some relevant concepts in cryptography is needed.

1. Cryptography

Cryptography is the study of techniques for secure communication in the presence of third parties called adversaries. One of its main applications in information security is protecting information from adversaries. Specifically, when applied to cryptocurrencies, it means that cryptography can be used to prove ownership of an asset, sign transactions, and secure communications.

The Bitcoin network utilizes cryptographic techniques to secure its network, protect wallet balances, create the authenticity of coins, and provide the required computational puzzle solutions needed for mining. There are three cryptographic techniques involved in bitcoin mining.

2. Hashing

The hashing function is a mathematical algorithm that maps data of any size to a bit string of a fixed size. Its main application in cryptocurrencies is mining. Normally, one would use the hashing function several times (referred to as double-hashing or hashing twice) to check the integrity of information, but it also has other applications in cryptography.

3. Mining

Transactions are bundled into blocks that are linked together to form a blockchain. The miner that first solves the cryptographic puzzle gets the privilege of putting the next block on the chain and receiving BTC as a reward (this is the concept of mining).

4. Blockchain

A blockchain is a continuously growing list of records, called blocks, which are linked and secured using cryptography. Each block typically contains a cryptographic hash of the previous block, a timestamp, transaction data (generally represented as a Merkle tree root hash), and the mining difficulty target.

Blockchain technology is what gives cryptocurrencies like Bitcoin their functionalities, including public/private key cryptography for authentication, a peer-to-peer networking protocol for decentralized consensus formation (mining), and self-contained digital assets. Thus, blockchain technology is responsible for processing transactions and is also responsible for enforcing the consensus protocol.

The Economics of Blockchain Technology and Crypto-Mining

At the core of Bitcoin and cryptocurrency mining is a fundamental economic concept called the tragedy of the commons, which William Forster Lloyd first introduced in his 1832 book titled "On the Law of Diminishing Returns as illustrated by the cases of Corn and Sheep." This idea states that shared resources (such as common pasture) will always be overexploited due to the incentive to choose personal gain over community loss. In short, each individual will have an incentive to maximize their benefit by adding livestock until the shared resource is completely depleted.

Bitcoin and cryptocurrency mining follow this economic concept. Because it is decentralized (i.e., there is no central authority), it requires computational power to function. Thus, a network-wide consensus must be achieved before any transactions can be validated and added to the public ledger (i.e., blockchain). This is done through a process called mining, in which miners continuously verify transactions on the network by solving complex cryptographic puzzles using their computing hardware until one of them finds the solution and wins the block. The miner that wins the block is rewarded with Bitcoin and transaction fees (this is the incentive).

However, the problem with this process is that it requires an increasing amount of effort as more miners join the network to solve these cryptographic puzzles. Thus, every 2,016 blocks (roughly every two weeks), the difficulty target associated with these puzzles is adjusted based on the network's recent performance to ensure that blocks are mined no faster than approximately every 10 minutes. If this happens, there will be fewer Bitcoin rewards for each block mined, and overall profits would decrease. However, if the opposite occurs and miners find solutions more quickly than expected, there will be a higher inflation rate, and overall profits will increase. This process is referred to as a hard fork, soft fork, or a change in protocol rules. Bitcoin's pricing and popularity have led it to account for more than 60% of the overall cryptocurrency market capitalization, with a total market cap of around $727.5 billion. Bitcoin's current pricing and mining difficulty level make it profitable for miners to dedicate significant amounts of computing power towards mining the cryptocurrency because they can expect to see a return on investment (ROI). The global average cost of mining one Bitcoin is $3,224.29, but this value can vary depending on the mining difficulty level in each country. Mining can be very profitable in regions where power is cheap, such as hydropower in Central America. However, in countries where power comes at a premium, such as China, mining can be less profitable or even loss-making.

Hardware and Overclocking

Miners typically join mining pools using their personal computers, but this has become extremely inefficient due to the tremendous amount of electricity Bitcoin mining requires. To resolve this problem, miners have started developing more sophisticated mining hardware to solve the puzzles quicker than their competitors and thus maximizing their profits by joining these pools.

This development is possible because Bitcoin uses an open-source algorithm that anyone can access, implement, and optimize through specialized software (i.e., mining software). Currently, two major types of hardware are used for mining: CPUs and GPUs. However, the latest trend is Field-Programmable Gate Array (FPGA) miners that can be customized for Bitcoin mining based on the available technology. Because Bitcoin and other cryptocurrency mining has grown so quickly in recent years, many individuals have started to build highly powerful mining rigs consisting of multiple GPUs to remain competitive. This has caused a shortage of graphics cards and led to their prices skyrocketing. Because so much computational power is required in the mining process, miners frequently use overclocking to increase the hash rate and solve these cryptographic puzzles faster.

Overclocking is the process of running a computer component at a speed that exceeds the manufacturer's recommendation, resulting in instability and ultimately damage the hardware. For example, manufacturers typically have recommended maximum operating temperatures for GPUs so they do not overheat while being pushed beyond their limits.

Although cryptocurrency mining has been popular in recent years, it has also become increasingly costly because of the amount of electricity used. In many cases, individuals will not be able to profit from mining due to the costs outweighing the benefits, and this has driven interest in alternative cryptocurrencies called altcoins that can still be mined using a regular computer's CPU or GPU.

Bitcoin produces a coin every 10 minutes on average until it reaches its predetermined limit of 21 million coins. Bitcoin must continue producing new blocks roughly every 10 minutes to maintain this inflation rate. This is why Bitcoin mining has become so critical to the cryptocurrency's ecosystem because, without a sufficient number of miners, the entire system would collapse.

If not enough people are mining Bitcoin to meet the demands of the network, the difficulty level associated with these cryptographic puzzles will decrease until it is manageable again for all miners. This is what happened in late 2013 when Bitcoin's price crashed from about $1,000 to below $500 causing many individual miners to stop mining because their costs exceeded the returns. This caused a decrease in supply and spurred an eventual increase in Bitcoin's price.

However, if too many individuals mine Bitcoin at once, the difficulty level will increase proportionally. This causes profitability to decrease for all but the most advanced and energy-efficient mining hardware. The same thing occurred in late 2017, with the price of cryptocurrency rising to unprecedented highs and a sudden influx of new miners. Therefore, profitable mining is a delicate balance between too many miners and not enough miners that can be easily disrupted by market fluctuations or advancements in hardware technology. This concept has been demonstrated recently as Bitcoin's difficulty level increased following reports from Bloomberg that Nvidia will be manufacturing specialized hardware for mining in the future. Furthermore, if Bitcoin's price continues to rise, more miners will likely join, especially when profitability is back at pre-crash levels. Consequently, the next wave of Bitcoin mining will most likely be driven by application-specific integrated chip (ASIC) miners who can significantly improve energy efficiency.

The economics of cryptocurrency mining is more complicated than initially perceived. Mining is more expensive, less profitable, and further from reaching mass adoption than one might expect. Therefore, the next step in cryptocurrency mining will not be a race to build out capacity as it is with traditional blockchain projects but a search for the most efficient hardware to mine a specific coin. It seems that ASICs will continue to reign supreme until more algorithms can offer significant improvements over PoW and PoS.

Profit and Return on Investment (ROI)

The main goal of mining is to generate rewards in the form of new Bitcoin issued into circulation. The reward mechanism is also referred to as "mining." This process involves adding transactions to the blockchain, which produces new blocks. New blocks are added to the blockchain by solving cryptographic puzzles through a mining process requiring significant processing power and electricity consumption. The first miner who solves these puzzles is rewarded with Bitcoin.

The following list shows the main factors that affect the profitability of Bitcoin mining:

1. Mining Difficulty

Mining difficulty is a relative measure of how difficult it is to find a new block. Mining difficulty is adjusted periodically as a function of how much hashing power the network of miners has deployed. In other words, it is a relative measure of how difficult it is to find a new block compared to the most recent blocks. Therefore, the more hashing power deployed on the network, the higher the difficulty and the more difficult it becomes to mine a new block. In addition, mining difficulty will arise when mining capacity is added to the network. So, for a miner to stay profitable, the Bitcoin price must keep up with the mining difficulty.

2. Mining Hardware's Performance

Mining hardware performance is measured in hashes per second, also referred to as mega-hashes per second (MH/s), kilo-hashes per second (KH/s), or giga-hashes per second (GH/s). The higher the number of hashes your mining hardware can perform, the faster you will be able to complete a block and the more likely you are to solve a cryptographic puzzle.

3. Electricity Costs

The main problem with mining is that it also consumes a lot of electricity, which turns into heat. The amount of heat generated by standard mining hardware is enormous and can often exceed 70 degrees Celsius (158°F). Therefore, large-scale mining operations are usually located in cold climates that can help keep the hardware temperature down.

4. Bitcoin's Exchange Rate

The only reason why anyone would want to buy a mining rig is for the prospect of making profits in Bitcoin or another cryptocurrency. Therefore, it is safe to assume that the price of Bitcoin influences most miners' plans. New miners will probably enter the market when Bitcoin's price rises, and existing miners will most likely expand their mining operations. This increased demand for hardware will drive up manufacturers' prices and increase the average cost of electricity in areas with surplus renewable energy (where electricity prices are low).

5. Cooling Requirements
Standard mining equipment also requires special ventilation to dissipate all the heat. If you opt for a custom-made PC specifically for mining, you will also need to purchase special case fans with ball bearings that can withstand high temperatures and constant usage.

6. Noise
Many people opt to run mining operations in their basements, where the noise won't disturb anyone. However, you should also consider that your neighbors will be able to hear it. Special ventilated enclosures with built-in cooling systems are available at online retailers and might be worth considering if you plan on running a mining operation in your home.

7. Availability of Mining Hardware
Currently, only a limited number of companies and individual miners produce mining hardware, which can affect its availability and increase its price due to supply and demand dynamics. This also leads to increased difficulty as the mining resources become scarcer. However, this problem is not evident

in cloud mining operations because you are renting mining resources from an established company. Your costs are based on the contract you sign with the operator, which means there is no risk of difficulty rising and no need to purchase expensive hardware.

8. Mining Pool

A mining pool is a group of miners who have decided to combine their computational power and split the rewards equally among all pool participants. Joining a mining pool can significantly increase your chance of finding blocks, although it will not make you immune to bad luck or other unexpected events. However, if you are considering investing in mining hardware, you should also consider joining a mining pool as it will increase your chances of making a profit.

When one of these factors changes in isolation, it does not mean miners will lose money immediately since they can simply switch their hashing power to mine another cryptocurrency, such as Litecoin or Ethereum. However, when multiple factors change at once, it is difficult for mining operations to remain profitable without making some changes, such as the location and/or cooling equipment.

Key Takeaways

- Mining operations require a lot of space, equipment, and electricity.
- Cryptocurrencies are mined because there is a high likelihood of earning profits from the mining process with the help of specialized hardware called ASICs.
- To be profitable, you need to consider several factors, including cost-efficiency and hardware and electricity costs.
- The price of Bitcoin significantly influences the profitability of mining operations.
- Mining operations also need to be set up in areas with low operating costs and abundant renewable energy sources such as wind and solar power.
- Make sure you have enough space for a high-density hardware installation and proper ventilation.
- Keep in mind that mining equipment will increase your electricity usage, leading to higher utility bills if you don't have a plan for this.

As you can see, running a profitable mining operation is not as straightforward as it might seem. There are several factors to consider and hundreds of possible scenarios you should explore before even thinking about investing in such an activity. Mining operations involve multiple considerations, including electricity costs, hardware costs, cooling systems, ventilation needs, and real estate requirements. Many of these factors are interrelated since mining hardware requires a lot of space to dissipate heat, increasing electricity costs and raising the need for cooling systems. We have also learned that it is important to look at your local electricity costs because they will be the determining factor when it comes to profitability.

Read on to find out the differences between solo and pool mining.

8

Solo vs. Pool Mining

Mining cryptocurrencies is all the rage right now. Whether you're mining Bitcoin, Litecoin, or just about any other altcoin out there, the chances are that your rig(s) will need to be constantly running to maximize your mining potential. There are two ways to mine coins: Solo Mining and Pool Mining. This chapter will explain the differences between both methods and why you should choose one over the other.

Introduction and the Theory behind Solo Mining and Pool Mining

Before we compare Solo Mining and Pool Mining, we first need to understand what they are and how they work. When mining on your own, you are essentially setting up your mining equipment to be run by a single computer, whether a regular desktop or a laptop. Your computer will try to solve computationally difficult problems with cryptographic hash functions used in the process of mining. When a problem is solved, this is called a block, and whoever found it gets awarded newly created Bitcoin (this is called mining).

Solo Mining

Solo mining is when you mine on your own without joining a pool. You set up your miner to connect to the Bitcoin network directly and to start hashing. The chance of you managing to mine a block by yourself is extremely low, around 1 in 100,000,000 with current difficulty levels. However, other coins have considerably lower difficulty levels, offering better chances at solo mining. The downside of this method is that if you do not manage to mine a block, all the time and effort spent setting up your miner would be wasted. To make mining worthwhile in terms of energy and time, it's best to join a mining pool.

Pool Mining

This method is when you join a group of other miners to increase your chances of successfully mining a block. By working as part of a pool, you will receive a share of the profits proportional to the effort you put in (this is called Proof-of-Work). However, the downside to this method is that your payouts will be vastly decreased because you will split the profits with others in the pool. A good example of a Bitcoin mining pool is Eligius. People who want to mine Bitcoin can join this particular pool because it follows the original payout structure of solo mining.

Comparing Solo Mining against Pool Mining: The Math and the Result

There are many variables when it comes to deciding between Solo Mining and Pool Mining. We will cover the most important ones and how they affect you as a miner.

1. Hash Rate

The main variable we need to look at is the mining pool's hash rate; this is how many calculations per second it can make. An example of this would be GHash.io which currently has approximately 44% of the market share. It does not necessarily mean that it has 44% of all the hash power, but it means that their pool will generate blocks more often than others. Mining pools like GHash.io are called "popular" because they have generated a lot of media attention (and members) which increases trust between miners and potential members to join their pool.

2. Hash Power = Block Finding Probability

In basic terms, the larger a pool is, the more likely it is to find a block. It does not necessarily mean that most pools can generate more money than solo miners with just as much hash rate, but it means you will have a better chance at receiving your payouts. You also want to look at the pool's variance, which is when you look at how stable it is. The bigger the pool, the smaller its variance and vice versa.

3. Payout Scheme

This is another important factor to consider. The profits are divided among all pool members according to how many "shares" they found. The more shares you have, the bigger your payout will be. However, a mining pool's hash rate determines what you can expect to get in terms of Bitcoin per day on average. Any time you find a block, the payout method is divided among all the members according to their invested shares.

4. Pool Fees

Pool fees are becoming more popular nowadays because they add value to mining in a pool or team up with big companies, especially for larger pools that own their equipment which requires maintenance. Fees are also used to prevent pool-hopping, which is when people hop between mining pools when they think that it will be profitable. You want to look for a percentage fee to not miss out on too much of your payout, although you should consider the amount of time it would take to receive your fair share at your hash rate. The lower the fee, the more profit you get. Solo miners usually don't even need to pay a fee because they can already keep the full payout.

5. Pool's Reputation and History

This is very important because it reassures miners that the pool owners cannot rip them off. This can be anything, including delays in payments, unclear returns on investment, or even not receiving any payments at all. Many other factors define a pool's reputation, and it is best to look for them before you even consider joining one. These factors include:

- Length of time the pool has been in service.
- History and reason for any downtime.
- Quality of the website, including speed, uptime, and overall appearance.
- Variance in the amount of hashing power they have.
- Payout schemes and associated fees.

6. Pool's User Interface

This is an important aspect because you will be looking at how user-friendly the website is. It should have statistics, graphs, and customizable options so you can monitor your mining progress. The only thing you need to be careful about is if the pool charges a fee for an upgraded user interface. If this is the case, you will want to consider a pool that does not charge a fee for a more professional-looking website. For solo mining, the only thing you should look for is a simple website with statistics on your mining progress.

7. Pools Location

The pool location will not matter because your mining rigs are working independently. This makes a slight difference because you want to get paid as fast as possible, and providers usually prioritize users from their own country. It shouldn't matter too much, but it is something to think about. Solo miners do not necessarily need to consider the location of the pool because you are your own "pool."

8. Pools Country and Workings behind It

This includes legal issues such as laws and the type of currency. You want to look for safe and reliable pools because the last thing you would want is to lose your earnings due to poor legalities. Examine how your pool works and what type of payment schemes they offer for various cryptocurrencies. You also want to know if you will be paid in Bitcoin. If the pool only deals with other cryptocurrencies, you might have to convert your earnings from Bitcoin before being able to withdraw them.

9. Electricity Costs

If you are located in a place where electricity costs are low, then solo mining would be the best option because you will make more money. You need to understand that if your electric bill is very high, you will end up spending more money on electricity than what you earn. This means that mining in a pool would be the best option because the fees involved will be less than what you earn. On the other hand, if your electric bill is very low and you don't mind spending more money on equipment, solo mining is the way ahead.

Key Factors of Mining - The Big Picture

Miners need to look at mining pools strategically because they are essentially working as a team which means you will get more consistent payouts, but the overall profits made by each member will be significantly lower than that of solo mining. When you look at the bigger picture, mining in a pool will always be more efficient than solo mining due to high hashes. A pool's location, reliability, reputation, and security are some of the most important factors that determine its viability. But you should always consider going solo if you have a very specific goal in mind which requires a large amount of money. If this is the case, then you should stick with solo mining.

Solo mining requires a lot of work, but the profits are higher because there are no fees. Although solo mining is more profitable, it also increases variance, which means you can potentially make significantly less money than pool mining even with the same equipment. It is ideal for people who want to mine Bitcoin as a hobby or those just stepping into the cryptocurrency world. But this is not ideal for people looking to make a living out of this. Mining pools are great for making money because they offer consistent payouts. But the disadvantage is that there are significant fees involved, and because of this, pool mining will always be less profitable than solo mining.

Miners should consider the key factors of both solo and pool mining because they ultimately determine the profitability and viability of your mining rig. You should also think about how much money and time you invested in your rig. You want to get the most out of your mining equipment, so you need to analyze both solo and pool mining so you can determine the most profitable option. The more informed you are about these factors, the more profitable you will be.

Solo or Pool? How to Decide against the Math

Whether solo mining or pool mining is more profitable depends on your situation. You will need to weigh your options against the combined factors mentioned above. This is not something you can decide on without doing any math or research because this will vary from one person to another. It all depends on how much money you want to spend on mining equipment, electricity costs, and personal expectations. You should do some research before committing to either solo or pool mining, whatever the case may be.

Most people who engage in cryptocurrency mining prefer mining pools even though it is less profitable than solo mining. But this is not something you should decide on without doing your own research and figuring out your needs and expectations. Mining pools help you earn consistent payouts, and this is very advantageous. You just need to weigh your options against the factors mentioned above. Solo mining offers higher profits, but this will entail a lot of up-front costs and hard work. You need to come up with an informed decision to balance your options against your budget and expectations.

Key Takeaways

- Solo mining is more profitable than pool mining with the same rig.
- You can make significantly more money from solo mining with a large amount of equipment.
- Mining pools are more profitable than solo mining when you factor in the costs of equipment and electricity.
- You need to weigh your options based on your situation, spending budget, and expectations.
- Mining pools are great for earning consistent payouts, but this requires significant fees.
- Solo mining offers more benefits than pool mining, but you need to spend a lot of money on equipment.

Although there are many variables to consider when choosing between Solo or Pool Mining, it seems that most people will choose to go for Pool Mining. Most mining pools have a good reputation and great community support. Assuming you already have a rig ready to mine, it may be easier for you to join an established mining pool rather than trying to set up your Solo Mining operation. Keep in mind that if you are part of a large mining pool, your chances of earning Bitcoins every single day are much higher than if you were trying to mine solo. This is because no matter how much hashing power you contribute, your impact on the total mining pool hashing power is relatively small.

Solo mining is always more profitable than pool mining. Pool mining will allow you to maximize your hashing power, but solo mining will increase profits significantly. Before making the decision, you need to weigh your options against each factor. Mining pools allow consistent payouts, but solo mining will increase profits significantly. In the end, it all depends on your situation, spending budget, and expectations.

The following chapter is about Proof of Work Coins and how you can get started!

9

Other Proof of Work Coins

As someone just getting into the world of cryptocurrencies, you may have concluded that there are way too many options on the market. You want to get in early and make a big profit, but you're not sure where to start. You've heard of Bitcoin, but it's simply too expensive now to invest in. Other coins are either scams or can't be mined by individuals. Some coins seem too complicated, and you're afraid of making the wrong choice. If only one coin met all your criteria, it would make things so much easier!

As it turns out, several coins can be mined by individuals. These are called "proof of work" coins, and they are the backbone of cryptocurrencies all over the world. This chapter aims to provide a simple guide for newcomers to start mining proof of work coins.

Proof of Work Coins

A proof of work coin is any digital currency that can be mined by anyone possessing basic computer hardware. This is the fundamental difference between proof of work coins and other coins on the market, such as Bitcoin or Litecoin. Other coins are "mined" with specialized equipment called ASICs (application-specific integrated circuits), which are pieces of hardware built strictly for mining cryptocurrencies like Bitcoin. With these new ASIC miners, the difficulty of mining Bitcoin has skyrocketed to such a degree that it can no longer be mined on a typical home computer.

Proof of work coins uses the same mining concepts as Bitcoin. They are mined through a process called hashing, which is performed by computer hardware. When calculating the total of a block, it is necessary to include all transactions. It takes some time for computers to calculate everything to prevent someone from adding fake transactions (also known as "spam") to trick you into thinking that they have more money than they do. Using proof of work coins, it takes an average user a certain amount of time to calculate a block. Once that block is calculated, it is broadcasted to the network and added to the blockchain. This prevents "spam" because if someone tried to add false transactions, they would have to recalculate the proof of work on all previous blocks for anything to happen.

Proof of work coins also generates new coins as a reward for the first people to calculate a given block. Once a proof of work coin is mined, it stays in circulation forever. Since there is no way to reset the mining difficulty, whoever makes the first calculation for a given block will always receive the reward. This is why it's possible to have an inflation system that increases the number of coins being mined over time while still staying true to the principles of a decentralized currency. This provides a way for everyone to trust that no one is cheating or stealing from anyone else.

Choosing a Coin to Mine

When you first start mining proof of work coins, it will take some time before you can mine a block successfully. Every coin has its algorithm for calculating the proof of work. This algorithm is based on two things: how easy it is to calculate and how many people are trying to perform that calculation at any given time.

If you want a coin to mine, you need to make sure it uses an algorithm that anyone with a computer can calculate. If multiple people are mining a coin simultaneously, specialized equipment (ASIC miners) is needed to come close to the number of coins generated by those with normal computers. ASICs do make mining much more profitable by increasing your hash rate (the number of calculations you can perform per second). However, it is usually not worth buying an ASIC unless you plan to mine a coin with a very high market value.

You should start mining by mining proof of work coins that use the following algorithms: SHA-256, Scrypt, or X11. All three of these algorithms can be calculated by CPUs (computer processors), which means anyone with a normal computer can easily mine them. Scrypt is also used for Litecoin, one of the most popular proofs of work coins in circulation.

Once you begin mining these types of coins, you will need to decide whether to mine solo or join a pool. Mining pools are groups of people who pool their resources together to increase their chances of successfully mining a block. Each pool will have its requirements, but most of them are pretty similar to the requirements for joining Bitcoin pools. Once you choose a pool, any rewards you get from successfully mining blocks are split between everyone who helped calculate the proof of work.

Once again, there are pros and cons to both solo and pool mining. In general, it's better to join a pool because the rewards are consistent, and you have a better chance of earning more. However, since each reward is split between everyone who helped calculate the proof of work, your share may sometimes be very small. Miners also take a cut from every reward to cover their costs (electricity, etc.), so you likely won't be earning as much as you would if you decided to mine solo.

A Step-by-Step Guide to Setting up Proof of Work Mining

1. Getting Started

The first thing you will need to do is download a "Wallet." A wallet lets you store, send, and receive any type of proof of work coin. To create a wallet, you will need to download the official software from the website of the cryptocurrency you want to mine. Once you have chosen your currency, visit its website or Github page for information on how to get started with mining it.

Once you have downloaded the program, you will be given a public key and a private key. The public key is what other users need to send you money or view your transaction history. You can also use the public key as an address when mining coins, which means anyone who knows your public key can help calculate the proof of work for any blocks you are currently trying to mine. The private key is a different password that allows you to access your wallet and money, so it should never be shared with anyone. The program will also ask you whether you want to encrypt your wallet - this ensures that no one can ever access your money if they ever get a hold of your computer / hard drive.

2. Calculating the Proof of Work

Once you've downloaded the wallet, it's time to start mining! The main screen within your wallet will tell you how many coins you have mined, how many blocks you've found, and how far away you are from successfully mining a block.

Once you click "Start," you will be asked to input a server that can calculate the proof of work for any blocks you want to mine. You usually have the choice between using the fastest server or one closest to you. You can also select "Show All" if you want to direct your computer to calculate the proof of work for all servers.

As soon as your computer successfully calculates the proof of work, it will start mining any blocks you are trying to mine. You can check the status of your mining by clicking "Tools" > "Mining." After you successfully calculate a proof of work, you will be able to see the coins you earned in your wallet.

Depending on how much computational power you have, you should see your coins increase by a small amount every few seconds. However, since this is proof of work mining, you may have to wait hours or even days for your coins to accumulate. In addition, if you are mining with a group of users, the number of coins you have mined might not correlate directly with your share of the reward.

3. Joining a Pool

Up to this point, you have been mining on your own. However, there are many benefits to joining an online pool of people trying to mine the same currency. For example, once you join a pool, you will see how your performance measures up to other users and work on calculating the proof of work.

One thing to be aware of is that since all rewards within a pool are split between everyone, your share of the reward may be very small. However, even if you are in a pool and working with other people, you still have a higher chance of successfully mining a block due to increased computational power.

The other big benefit of joining a pool is that you can often receive daily payouts. While mining alone usually only rewards you once the mined block is confirmed, joining a pool guarantees daily payouts to everyone working within the pool.

Key Takeaways

- To start mining, you will need to download the official software from the website of the cryptocurrency you want to mine.
- After installing the software, you will be given a public key and a private key. The public key is what other users need to send you money or view your transaction history. You can also use the public key as an address when mining coins.
- The private key is a different password that allows you to access your wallet and money, so it should never be shared with anyone.
- The program will also ask you whether you want to encrypt your wallet - this ensures that no one can ever access your money if they ever get a hold of your computer / hard drive.
- Once you've downloaded the wallet, it's time to start mining! The main screen within your wallet will tell you how many coins you have mined, how many blocks you've found, and how far away you are from successfully mining a block.

Mining proof of work coins is a great way to get started in cryptocurrency and learn how it all works behind the scenes. Although solo mining can be profitable, you should join a pool if you want to increase your chances of successfully mining coins. Since all proof of work coins are based on public-key cryptography, it's also a great way to learn more about how this technology works. Once you become familiar with the process of mining proof of work coins, you can easily mine other coins in the future.

Read on to understand more about risks with cryptocurrency.

10

Criticisms and Risks

In the last decade, cryptocurrency has become a hot topic. Especially since the price spike of Bitcoin in late 2017, more and more people have become interested in cryptocurrency. However, this interest has brought about fear, uncertainty, and doubt from the public about how cryptocurrencies actually work. This is not helped by those with a vested interest in discouraging people from getting into cryptocurrencies, like banks or credit card companies. One of the major things people are confused about is how mining cryptocurrency works.

Mining is the process of verifying and validating transactions on the blockchain. By mining, individuals worldwide verify transactions on a distributed ledger to ensure that no fraud is occurring. Mining requires a lot of computing power and energy, so critics claim that mining cryptocurrency is wasteful and not sustainable in the long term. This chapter seeks to address these concerns by looking at the criticisms of mining from a technical perspective and how society can mitigate these risks.

The Risks and Drawbacks of Crypto-Mining: A Technical Perspective

The mining process for Bitcoin and other cryptocurrencies has been heavily criticized. There are many concerns about how it uses up energy and how wasteful it is. There are also concerns about the centralization of mining due to the rise of mining pools and larger companies that can afford to mine faster than any individual. This leads to the power being mostly concentrated in the hands of a few people, which threatens the decentralized nature of the blockchain. These are the main concerns of mining, according to critics:

1. Mining Is Wasteful and Unsustainable

One of the major criticisms of crypto-mining is that it uses so much energy and resources. Mining takes a lot of computing power and electricity. Critics argue that that leads to mining costing more than the actual value of Bitcoin or other cryptocurrencies. This criticism points out that unscrupulous companies have used crypto-mining to defraud investors as proof that it is an unsustainable practice. In Iceland, the process of crypto-mining has even been linked to increases in energy costs and power shortages.

2. Centralization of Mining Threatens Decentralized Nature of Blockchains

Critics argue that mining pools have also contributed to centralizing control over how cryptocurrency operates. This is seen as a threat because blockchains are supposed to be immutable and decentralized. However, mining pools have created more issues surrounding this by giving those who run the pool more power. The biggest problem with this is that it still allows for the possibility of miners colluding together to increase their profits at the cost of other people on the blockchain, which can lead to double-spending or faulty transactions that could hold up transactions on the blockchain.

3. Mining Is Expensive and Inaccessible to Most People

Due to the necessary equipment needed for mining, critics argue that it is a practice aimed at people who have a lot of money to invest in mining rigs. This means that cryptocurrency will always be confined to existing within a small group of people, and, as a result, many individuals won't find it profitable to mine. This is because the initial cost of mining rigs can be prohibitively expensive for most investors due to the high price point of these machines.

4. Threats of Hacking and Centralization

There are risks associated with hacking mining pools for cryptocurrencies, which are seen as dangerous to the industry. While there have not been any cases of hackers taking over or hacking cryptocurrency mining pools so far, this has opened up a debate about the security surrounding these systems. Mining pools have also become targets for Distributed Denial of Service (DDoS) attacks, where individuals who do not like the aims of mining pools can bring down their services in an attempt to disrupt operations.

5. Mining Pools Disadvantage Small Miners

The growing number of mining pools is seen as a barrier for people who mine with less sophisticated equipment or on a smaller scale. This is because mining pools require users to have more processing power which means they are not accessible for people who cannot buy the right equipment or cannot compete with big-scale investors.

6. Mining May Be Illegal in Some Countries

Some countries have banned Bitcoin and other cryptocurrencies due to their unregulated and anonymous nature. In China, one of the first countries to ban cryptocurrency trading and ICOs, mining also became illegal as a result. This law aimed to discourage any activity related to cryptocurrencies because it could create issues with their ability to track transactions and collect taxes from businesses involved in trading.

7. Mining Is Not Profitable for Most People

Due to the number of issues with crypto-mining, critics argue that the costs involved in doing this outweigh any potential profits. As a result, mining may not be profitable for most individuals, and they would be better off spending their money in other ways. This is especially true in the current market, where there has been a decline in cryptocurrency prices, and people are still waiting to see if the market will recover.

8. Mining Is Not an Equal Opportunity

Miners can decide whether they want to mine a certain cryptocurrency in a way that hurts smaller coins. This is especially true in cases where mining pools focus on one or two specific cryptocurrencies over others because people may choose not to invest in those simply because there are too many mining pools for that specific coin. This can create an uneven playing field where cryptocurrencies are not being mined in the same way, which could cause issues with price and how it is maintained on the market.

9. Decreased Efficiency

Critics argue that mining is not an efficient way to manage a cryptocurrency. Miners have to dedicate energy and computational power to solve hashes in proof-of-work cryptocurrencies. This can be done by using more powerful computers or adding extra hardware to their existing machines. However, some critics argue that the investment is too much for what they get in return because it uses up a lot of energy for very little reward.

10. The Slow Process of Mining

Cryptocurrency mining is a slow process that can only do one thing at a time. A new block can only be mined after the previous one has been completed, which limits how quickly cryptocurrency transactions can be completed. This is seen as a disadvantage because transactions need to be validated before they are added to the blockchain.

11. Proof-of-Stake Mining Is Preferred over Proof-of-Work

As proof of stake is a faster mining system compared to proof of work, critics argue that this system is preferred as there are fewer costs involved, and it can be done from home instead of requiring high-level processing power and hardware. With proof of stake, users are not required to use up electricity for processing power that does not bring in any returns.

12. Mining Creates Waste

When cryptocurrencies are mined, they often go through several intermediaries before the final transaction is reached. Each of these steps needs computing power and energy, which means there is a lot of waste in cryptocurrency mining. Critics argue that this wastes a lot of time and money as well as electricity.

13. Mining Includes a High Level of Risk

When miners look to invest in cryptocurrencies, they need to consider the risk factor associated with them. Unlike other investments, cryptocurrency mining has a high level of risk because there is no guarantee that the coin will hold its value, something that other investments may be able to provide.

14. The Energy Costs Outweigh the Profit

Critics argue that electricity costs outweigh mining profits, especially in recent times as a result of the decline in cryptocurrency prices. In the current market, critics argue that mining costs are almost as much as the profits or that it incurs a loss, and this doesn't make it worthwhile for most people to dedicate their time and money to do this.

In short, cryptocurrency mining has been subject to a lot of criticism in recent times because several factors work against it. There are many instances where people argue that mining is dangerous and can cause damage to the environment. On top of this, there are concerns over energy costs and how this cost outweighs the profit that can be made due to a decline in cryptocurrency prices. However, mining is still considered profitable for some people because it is a relatively cheap way to get cryptocurrencies.

How Society and the Market Can Mitigate These Risks

Some steps can be taken to reduce or mitigate the risks of mining. Here are a few things you can do to help society and the market:

1. Use Renewable Energy Sources

Miners can use renewable energy sources to reduce the risk of mining. This will offset the effects of mining on the environment while also reducing costs. This is a win-win situation for miners and society at large, especially as renewable energy sources are becoming more affordable in recent times.

2. Create Better Mining Facilities

Mining facilities can be built to use less power, which means they impact the environment. Miners can also build data centers that use renewable energy to offset environmental damage. They can also use robotics and other technology to reduce the cost of labor, which would also reduce their expenses and those for society at large.

3. Create Less Polluting Cryptocurrencies

Some cryptocurrencies don't require mining because they use alternative methods. Alternative currencies can run on platforms that don't require such high-level computing power, reducing the risks associated with cryptocurrency mining.

4. Create Carbon Offsets

Carbon offsets are another way of reducing the risks of mining because they allow miners to contribute to environmental conservation. This means that the carbon emissions caused by mining would be offset because of something else, like investing in eco-friendly projects. This would reduce costs and harmful effects on the environment and allow miners to offset their impact while also providing benefits for society.

5. Adopt Sustainable Mining Practices

Miners can adopt sustainable mining practices to reduce the harmful effects of their activities on the environment. For example, they can recycle water instead of draining it out. They can also recycle the heat produced during mining operations to reduce energy costs and pollution. A lot of miners are already adopting such practices, and this is a good sign for the market.

6. Contribute to Research and Development Projects

Miners can contribute to research and development projects that would reduce the harmful effects of mining on society as a whole. For example, they can help develop the latest renewable energy technology, which would reduce the environmental impact of mining. This can be done by investing in research and development projects or through sponsoring such initiatives.

7. Encourage More Efficient Mining Software

Miners can encourage the development of more efficient mining software that uses less power and doesn't damage the environment. This will significantly reduce energy costs and offset harmful environmental effects. Currently, companies are working on more efficient mining software, which would be beneficial for the market in the long term.

8. Encourage Mining Pools

Miners can encourage mining pools, which are shared spaces used for mining. This is very different from solo mining, which is when a miner operates an independent machine. Mining pools are much more efficient because they allow miners to team up and share resources, reducing costs and harmful effects on the environment. This also increases profits for miners since it would allow them to mine more efficiently.

9. Support Non-Profit Initiatives

Miners can support non-profit initiatives aimed at reducing the environmental impact of mining. Those organizations will use the funds for clean energy projects, recycling programs, or other initiatives that aim to reduce harmful environmental effects. Miners should also avoid mining cryptocurrencies without any economic plan because this will cause a lot of trouble for the market, and it could even lead to the collapse of some currencies.

Key Takeaways

- Bitcoin and other cryptocurrencies are created through a process called mining.
- Miners use special software to solve mathematical problems in order to create new coins.
- Many people have criticized the environmental impact of cryptocurrency mining.
- Miners can adopt sustainable practices to reduce the harmful effects of their activities on the environment.
- They can also contribute to research and development projects that would reduce the harmful effects of mining on society as a whole.
- Miners should avoid mining cryptocurrencies with a high energy consumption because this will be very costly.
- Miners can support non-profit initiatives that are aimed at reducing the environmental impact of mining.

Energy-related costs are causing concern among cryptocurrency miners because they outweigh the potential profits made through mining. However, there are many steps miners can take to reduce their impact on the environment and society as a whole. These steps include using renewable energy, minimizing carbon emissions, using sustainable mining practices, encouraging more efficient mining software, and developing better infrastructure such as data centers. By taking these steps, miners can save money while also mitigating the risks of mining.

Conclusion

"Learning how cryptocurrency works is like learning a new language. It is incredibly difficult at the beginning, but once it clicks, it will stick with you forever."

— Olawale Daniel

There's a very common misconception about cryptocurrency mining, and that is that it's merely a process to generate new coins. However, this is not entirely the case. A great part of cryptocurrency mining involves verifying transactions on a blockchain network and adding them to a distributed ledger. The process also safeguards against double-spending of a distributed ledger. Cryptocurrencies have similar dynamics to fiat money because the transactions must be debited from one account and credited to a different one. The main problem with cryptocurrency is that it is easy to manipulate. This is why only verified miners can update the distributed ledger on

Bitcoin. This means that miners are the ones in control of preventing double-spending.

The network creates new coins during the mining process and rewards them to the miners as compensation for their efforts. Since this is a decentralized currency lacking a central authority, the mining process is a vital step in validating the transactions. The rewards serve as incentives to keep the miners working to secure the network.

The great thing about this book is it isn't like any other book on the market. It provides hands-on instructions on how to get involved in the crypto mining world. It's also very easy to follow because it explains complex concepts in an interesting, simple manner. This book is ideal for beginners and experienced miners alike.

Now that you read this book, you should have a very good idea of the world of crypto mining. You understand the proof-of-work mechanism and how it differs from the proof-of-stake consensus protocol. This book also covers the pros and cons of each mechanism in-depth, allowing you to determine the right coins to mine for your needs. You are now very familiar with the various mining strategies and can easily set up your GPU for mining. Chapter 3c also introduces new alternatives in case you don't want to be mining from home.

In chapter 4a, you have come across invaluable information regarding how you can set up your own mining rig at home. This chapter also delves deep into the economics of mining, providing you with a better understanding of how the numbers and calculations are run. Now that you have read this chapter, you must be aware of how you can maintain your mining income.

The following chapters describe the difference between solo mining and pool mining. They also help you determine the best option for you by offering the calculations of each. In case you decide to go for pooling mining, the chapter provides information on how you can find and prepare a pool account and how you can mine Monero, Litercoin, or other PoW coins. The book also teaches you the risks of crypto mining and familiarizes you with the criticisms surrounding the topic.

Having read this book, you are now fully prepared to embark on your crypto mining journey. It is finally time to earn passive income and make money from mining Bitcoin and other altcoins.

References

Hong, E. (2022, February 15). How does bitcoin mining work? Retrieved from Investopedia website: https://www.investopedia.com/tech/how-does-bitcoin-mining-work/

Freeman, J. B. (2020, November 14). Mining explained: A detailed guide on how cryptocurrency mining works. Retrieved from Freeman Law website: https://freemanlaw.com/mining-explained-a-detailed-guide-on-how-cryptocurrency-mining-works/

Chandler, S. (2021, December 16). Proof of work is at the core of the system that manages Bitcoin transactions and secures the network. Retrieved from Business Insider website: https://www.businessinsider.com/personal-finance/proof-of-work

What is a node in a cryptocurrency network? Examples. (2018, February 23). Retrieved from Market Business News website: https://marketbusinessnews.com/financial-glossary/node-cryptocurrency-network/

Public and private keys: What are they? (n.d.). Retrieved from Gemini website: https://www.gemini.com/cryptopedia/public-private-keys-cryptography

PricewaterhouseCoopers. (n.d.). Blockchain: A new tool to cut costs. Retrieved from PwC website: https://www.pwc.com/m1/en/media-centre/articles/blockchain-new-tool-to-cut-costs.html

Block reward. (n.d.). Retrieved from PCMAG website: https://www.pcmag.com/encyclopedia/term/block-reward

Antonovici, A. (2021, June 28). Dogecoin mining 2021: Everything you need to know. Retrieved from Yahoo Finance website: https://finance.yahoo.com/news/dogecoin-mining-2021-everything-know-213659431.html

Binance Academy. (2018, December 3). ASIC-resistant. Retrieved from Binance Academy website: https://academy.binance.com/en/glossary/asic-resistant

Daly, L. (2021, September 24). What is proof of stake (PoS) in crypto? Retrieved from The Motley Fool website: https://www.fool.com/investing/stock-market/market-sectors/financials/cryptocurrency-stocks/proof-of-stake/

Floyd, D. (2021, November 17). How do you mine litecoin? Retrieved from Investopedia website: https://www.investopedia.com/tech/how-do-you-mine-litecoin/

Frankenfield, J. (2022, February 7). Proof-of-Stake (PoS). Retrieved from Investopedia website: https://www.investopedia.com/terms/p/proof-stake-pos.asp

Gondek, C. (n.d.). What is Ethereum, and what are its use cases? Retrieved from Originstamp.com website: https://originstamp.com/blog/what-is-ethereum-and-what-are-its-use-cases/

Laura, M. (2021, September 18). The best coin to mine - your best Altcoin mining choices. Retrieved from BitDegree.org Crypto Exchanges website: https://www.bitdegree.org/crypto/tutorials/best-coin-to-mine

McIntyre, V. A. P. by. (2019, October 7). Why proof of stake is less secure than proof of work. Retrieved from Etherplan website: https://etherplan.com/2019/10/07/why-proof-of-stake-is-less-secure-than-proof-of-work/9077/

(N.d.). Retrieved from Softwaretestinghelp.com website: https://www.softwaretestinghelp.com/cryptocurrency-to-mine-with-gpu/#:~:text=Bitcoin%20is%20still%20the%20most,An%20example%20is%20Nicehash.

Bitcoin mining. (2020, July 17). Retrieved from Corporate Finance Institute website: https://corporatefinanceinstitute.com/resources/knowledge/other/bitcoin-mining/

Hamilton, D. (2020, February 4). Ethereum Mining vs. Bitcoin Mining: Which is More Profitable? Retrieved from CoinCentral website: https://coincentral.com/ethereum-mining-vs-bitcoin-mining-which-is-more-profitable/

Laura, M. (2021, October 20). How to mine cryptocurrency: Beginner's guide to crypto mining. Retrieved from BitDegree.org Crypto Exchanges website: https://www.bitdegree.org/crypto/tutorials/how-to-mine-cryptocurrency

Reiff, N. (2021, December 3). Bitcoin vs. Ethereum: What's the difference? Retrieved from Investopedia website: https://www.investopedia.com/articles/investing/031416/bitcoin-vs-ethereum-driven-different-purposes.asp

Can I use my new gaming PC to mine cryptocurrency? (n.d.). Retrieved from Quora website: https://www.quora.com/Can-I-use-my-new-gaming-PC-to-mine-cryptocurrency

Kingston, C. (2022, January 1). Mining Bitcoin with your gaming PC: The ultimate 2022 guide. Retrieved from Black Belt Gamer website: https://blackbeltgamer.com/mining-bitcoin-with-your-gaming-pc/

NiceHash - leading cryptocurrency platform for mining and trading. (n.d.-a). Retrieved from Nicehash.com website: https://www.nicehash.com/support/general-help/nicehash-service/what-is-nicehash-and-how-it-works

NiceHash - leading cryptocurrency platform for mining and trading. (n.d.-b). Retrieved from Nicehash.com website: https://www.nicehash.com/blog/post/nicehash-quickminer-complete-guide

NiceHash - leading cryptocurrency platform for mining and trading. (n.d.-c). Retrieved from Nicehash.com website: https://www.nicehash.com/blog/post/why-should-i-start-mining-with-nicehash

About — Compass. (n.d.). Retrieved from Compass Mining Inc website: https://compassmining.io/about

Compass. (2021, July 18). How to start mining bitcoin: A step-by-step guide. Retrieved from Newsroom – Compass website: https://compassmining.io/education/five-steps-how-to-start-mining-bitcoin/

Compass mining objective review: Pros and cons. (n.d.). Retrieved from Lynalden.com website: https://www.lynalden.com/compass-mining/

Thank you. Please consider writing a review.

www.ingramcontent.com/pod-product-compliance
Lightning Source LLC
Chambersburg PA
CBHW071253050326
40690CB00011B/2376